VIRTUAL REALITY IN CURRICULUM AND PEDAGOGY

Virtual Reality in Curriculum and Pedagogy explores the instructional, ethical, practical, and technical issues related to the integration of immersive virtual reality (VR) in school classrooms. The book's original pedagogical framework is informed by qualitative and quantitative data collected from the first-ever study to embed immersive VR in secondary school science, ICT, and drama classrooms. Students and scholars of technology-enhancing learning, curriculum design, and teacher education alike will find key pedagogical insights into leveraging the unique properties of VR for authentic, metacognitive, and creative learning.

Erica Southgate is Associate Professor of Emerging Technologies for Education in the School of Education at the University of Newcastle, Australia, and Lead Researcher of the VR School Research Project.

DIGITAL GAMES, SIMULATIONS, AND LEARNING

While clearly the use of games for supporting education is not new, the use of digital games is comparatively recent. With the emergence of web-based services, increased broadband and the growth of online communities, the use of digital games presents us with a unique set of engaging tools and techniques, based upon game mechanics such as competition, narrative, missions and quests.

Increasingly games are being seen not as a technology but as a cultural form with its own genres, be they casual games played by everyone, serious games played to learn and engage or gamification whereby game elements are used to reach new audiences. Games offer us new toolsets that can be used effectively in activities as wide-ranging as therapy, awareness-raising or marketing as well as more conventional curricula. The versatility of digital games to be applied to any problem or challenge has gained games new cultural status that they did not have previously. Digital educational games seek to inform, educate and motivate learners and to extend the range of our ability to learn in classrooms by making the world our classroom and by putting social interaction rather than curriculum objectives at the centre of the learner's experience.

Game science is evolving, too, and game mechanics are just beginning to transform education and how it is produced and how learning is assessed, with real potential for providing just-in-time learning and supporting hard-to-reach learner groups. However the growth and spread of digital games in educational contexts is still relatively in its infancy and the best methods for developing, assessing and deploying these approaches are also in their earliest stages of advancement. This book series thus aims, primarily, to bring existing game theory and practices together to support the ongoing development of game science as a sub-disciplinary and cross-disciplinary academic body of evidence, as a methodology of investigation, and as a set of tools and approaches, methods and frameworks for learning.

While game science has the power to transcend normal silos of disciplines, the academic communities in different disciplines and in different continents have had too few opportunities to work as an interdiscipline, in part because the field is so new and research has been taking place in such diverse disciplinary, sectoral and international contexts. This book series therefore specifically aims to build bridges between diverse research, teaching, policy and learner communities and is inspired by the next generation of young researchers currently completing their early studies in the field. Towards this end, the series brings together leading theorists, thinkers and practitioners into a community of practice around the key themes and issues of digital games and learning. These theorists come from areas as diverse as health and well-being, business and innovation, education, computer science and engineering to name a few. Their perspectives include views from professional practice as well as as from theoretical perspectives.

It is important not to underestimate the scale of the work ahead in this new field, but it is also important to recognise the power of these new tools beyond our current understanding of what they can do or will do in the future. Games will always be a central part of early-stage learning, but now the capability of games to save lives, to inform citizens and to contribute positive outcomes socially are just beginning to be understood. We have always understood the power of games to entertain: this series shows us scientifically how the power of play can be harnessed for more profound purposes, more altruistic reasons in new forms of sustainable and scalable education. *Digital Games and Learning* will explore the lineaments of the new learning, and will reveal how and in what contexts that learning will take shape.

Professor Sara de Freitas Coventry University, Coventry, UK
Professor Paul Maharg The Australian National University, Canberra, Australia. June 2013.

Series Editors Sara de Freitas and Paul Maharg
Digital Games and Learning by Nicola Whitton
Aesthetics and Design for Game-based Learning by Michele D. Dickey
Online Gaming and Playful Organization by Harald Warmelink
Serious Play edited by Catherine Beavis, Michael Dezuanni, and Joanne O'Mara
Game Science in Hybrid Learning Spaces by Sylvester Arnab
Virtual Reality in Curriculum and Pedagogy by Erica Southgate

VIRTUAL REALITY IN CURRICULUM AND PEDAGOGY

Evidence from Secondary Classrooms

Erica Southgate

Routledge
Taylor & Francis Group

NEW YORK AND LONDON

First published 2020
by Routledge
52 Vanderbilt Avenue, New York, NY 10017

and by Routledge
2 Park Square, Milton Park, Abingdon, Oxon OX14 4RN

Routledge is an imprint of the Taylor & Francis Group, an informa business

Library of Congress Cataloging-in-Publication Data
A catalog record for this title has been requested

ISBN: 978-0-367-26202-0 (hbk)
ISBN: 978-0-367-26200-6 (pbk)
ISBN: 978-0-429-29198-2 (ebk)

Typeset in Bembo
by Taylor & Francis Books

To Teresa whose love sees me through the best and worst of times.

CONTENTS

ILLUSTRATIONS

Figures

Tables

ACKNOWLEDGEMENTS

This book would not have been possible without the commitment, tenacity, and invaluable contribution of the students, teachers, and school leaders of Callaghan College and Dungog High School. Thanks to my family, Jo, Stew, Georga, and Sean, who are unwavering in their support of my endeavours. Power to all those women in academia, the teaching profession, and the technology industry whose accomplishments are often diminished or overlooked but who continue to fight against all forms of discrimination – you inspire me.

1

INTRODUCTION

From the Germ of an Idea to a Gem of an Idea (or How This Book Came About)

In August 2016, I met with teachers from the junior high school campuses of Callaghan College to brainstorm a project that would use highly immersive virtual reality (iVR) in classrooms. By chance, a few months earlier, I had sat next to the principal of Callaghan College and we had struck up a conversation about technology and learning. I discussed the newly commercially released Oculus Rift, describing the wonders of fully interactive virtual reality (VR) that transported users to amazing environments like no other technology and which, in some cases, even allowed students to create their own unique worlds to demonstrate mastery of learning objectives. I told him that I wanted to do research on using the technology in schools but was unsure what the research would look like because putting high-end VR in classrooms was relatively untested. I had a germ of an idea with no funding to resource its development, and high-end VR was (and still is) expensive, especially for low-income school communities like Callaghan College. Unperturbed, the Callaghan College team worked tirelessly to progress the VR School Study. Over the following two years, a participatory research project unfolded, gradually sharpening its focus on using highly iVR in science and technology classrooms. In 2018, the study was expanded to include a performing arts class at rural Dungog High School.

While there were several decades of educational research on using screen-based VR (delivered via desktop computers or mobile devices), and teachers had been experimenting with Google Expeditions since 2014, research on using iVR (VR delivered via a head mounted display or headset) in schools was (and is) only just emerging. When the VR School Study began there were no research or practical models to draw upon. We needed to imagine, invent, and problem-solve what using high-end iVR – with its spatial requirements, ethical and safety implications, and unique pedagogical potential – might look like in low-income school communities. It was, to quote a teacher from the Callaghan College study, an 'arduous' journey.

It was precisely the 'ups and downs' of the research journey that have yielded the most valuable findings. The aim of this book is to stimulate a deeper conversation about the pedagogical value of iVR by sharing insights into what happens when you take this emerging technology out of the controlled conditions of a laboratory and put it into the dynamic natural setting of the school. This is a story that is far removed from the evangelism that permeates the EdTech space. This book offers an evidence-informed narrative in the tradition of critical studies of technology in education. Selwyn (2008) articulates a fundamental premise of the critical stance when he argues that far more attention should be paid to the 'state-of-the-actual' in the field educational technology rather than the 'state-of-the-art' (p. 83). This means moving away from a position of trying to 'prove' a technology is good for learning to scrutinising what is 'actually taking place when technology meets classroom', especially from the perspectives of teachers and students and in settings that do not fit the well-resourced 'model' schools in which technologies are often tested (Selwyn, 2008, p. 83).

Adopting a critical position when researching educational technology does not involve stymieing enthusiasm, curiosity, or a spirit of adventure. Rather, it is about maintaining a disposition of passionate distance: The joy and engagement that a technology can bring into classrooms should not be confused with the need to understand, through rigorous inquiry, its myriad implications and complications for diverse groups of learners and their teachers. Passionate distance involves honestly and credibly accounting for a technology's impact on an intricate, interrelated set of individual and social dynamics influenced by curriculum and pedagogical context and technical capability.

Technical Terms Explained

There are a number of technical terms which appear regularly in this book. The first is *virtual reality* (VR) which refers to a 3D computer-generated environment which can be a highly imaginative or an accurate simulation of something in the real world. VR can be experienced via a computer or mobile device screen, a CAVE (a room that surrounds the user with projection screens), or a head mounted display (HMD) commonly called a VR headset.

In scholarly circles, VR that is delivered or mediated via a headset and has positional tracking is called immersive virtual reality (iVR) (Slater and Sanchez-Vives, 2016). The term iVR is used to differentiate it from screen-based VR. iVR hardware includes motion tracking systems which detect the orientation of a user. *Positional tracking* can be 'outside-in' (that is the position of the user's headset is tracked by sensors/cameras which are positioned in the room) or 'inside-out' (that is the position of the user headset is tracked by sensors/cameras within the headset itself). In addition, different iVR equipment allows for different *degrees of freedom* (DoF) of movement and this affects interaction and navigation opportunities within a virtual environments. DoF denotes the number of ways an object can move through 3D space (Google, 2019). To simplify, some VR headsets allow for 3DoF which means that tracking accounts for whether a user's head is moving forward/backward, up/down, or left/right. Other (higher-end) headsets allow for 6DoF which means that in addition to 3DoF, the head's rotational movements of pitch, yaw, and roll are tracked. 6DoF hardware allows for a greater range of interaction and navigation opportunities in a virtual environment usually generating a more immersive experience.

From a hardware perspective there are a range of headsets available. These include 3DoF headsets designed to have smartphones slide into the front of them with the combination of phone and headset producing the iVR experience. Some of these headsets are handheld while others are fitted with a head strap, and some have handheld controllers that enable navigation and interaction in the virtual environment. Some high-end VR headsets are 'tethered' or attached with a cable to a computer that has powerful graphics capacity. These have sophisticated 'outside-in' tracking systems external to the headset and controllers that usually allow for 6DoF navigation and (gestural) interaction in virtual environments. Recently, 'stand-alone' or 'all-in-one' headsets have been released. These wireless headsets have the computing power to run iVR in the headset and do not require an external computer. The positional tracking is 'inside-out' coming from the headset itself rather than external sensors. This type of equipment also has controllers. Some of these 'stand-alone' headsets offer 3DoF (e.g. Oculus Go headset) while others offer 6DoF (e.g. Oculus Quest or Vive Focus headsets).

Depending on the combination of hardware and software application and the DoF, there can be different modes of *interaction* for selection and manipulation of virtual objects and *navigation* in virtual environments. For example in gaze-based applications, users look at objects or hotspot for pop-ups to activate and/or for teleporting travel to occur. Controllers that come with headsets can allow for ray-casting (or point and pick up) interaction and teleporting in some applications, while more sophisticated gestural controllers with 6DoF hardware provide virtual hands to use in some applications. In 2020 hand tracking technology will come to high-end iVR systems so that controllers will no longer be required for all applications: A person's natural hands will be used to pick and manipulate virtual objects opening up the medium to people who are not comfortable with mechanical controllers.

The combination of iVR headset, tracking systems, and software applications can create a feeling of actually being in a virtual environment – when you put the headset on, it's not like looking at a movie on a screen, it's like being in a movie and, in some cases, you can enact your own plot. The term *immersion* is key to understanding iVR. Immersion reflects the technical capabilities of a system to approximate movement and interaction in a virtual environment while the intense sense of actually 'being there' in a virtual environment is called *presence* (Slater and Wilbur, 1997). In networked VR such as multi-player computer games (also called multi-user virtual environments [MUVEs]), the feeling of 'being there with others' is called *co-presence* (Slater and Sanchez-Vives, 2016).

The primary focus of this book is iVR although it is sometimes just referred to this as VR. iVR covers a variety of experiences. These range from those where a seated user can passively look around at an environment to more 'bounded' tour experiences that involve guided navigation and interaction to fully realised (seemingly endless) virtual worlds and studio environments that provide the user with a high degree of agency and autonomy through navigation, manipulation, interaction, verbal and non-verbal communication, creative activity, and free play by oneself and sometimes with others. This latter type of VR is sometimes called highly immersive virtual reality (highly iVR). The VR School Study, detailed in chapters 4, 5, 6, and 7, was an exploration of learning using highly iVR, specifically 'sandbox' applications which included content creation tools for users without the need to 'code-to-create' in a virtual world.

Interaction in all types of VR is often mediated through an *avatar*. An avatar is a virtual representation of the user in human, animal, cartoon, or icon form. Users can often customise their avatar's appearance and sometimes even modes of interaction. Depending on the type of virtual environment, a person's avatar can interact with other user's avatars or 'non-player characters' which are computer controlled characters, for example the livestock which populate the game Minecraft. In some virtual environments, a user can have first person viewpoint; that is, they can see through the eyes of their avatar and interact in the environment as the avatar. Alternatively, users can have a third person view in which they adopt a 'disembodied' perspective where the user has a removed view of objects, characters, and action but may still be able to control an avatar and elements of the virtual environment (Gorisse, Christmann, Amato, and Richir, 2017).

In some virtual environments, users can switch between first and third person viewpoints, and this can help some people experience less *cybersickness*, a condition that has symptoms similar to motion sickness (headache, nausea and dizziness, and clamminess) (Rebenitsch and Owen, 2016). While there are a number of theories about why people can get cybersick in VR, and technical solutions to mitigate this, educators should be aware that it is difficult to predict if a student will have an adverse reaction (see chapter 5).

A central concept in this book is *learning affordance*. In the technology field, the term affordance refers to the actual or perceived properties or attributes of a thing which suggest to a user how it might be interacted with (Kaptelinin and Nardi, 2012). Extending on this, the term learning affordance has been used to refer to the action potential (utility) of a technology for learning (Bower, 2008). To apply this to VR, learning affordances are specific properties or attributes within a virtual environment that suggest or allow for certain learning tasks or type of learning to occur (Dalgarno and Lee, 2010). For example, the 3D affordance of virtual environments can enhance a learner's knowledge of spatial concepts (chapter 2 outlines this concept in detail). The learning affordance perspective recognises that the technology itself does not necessarily cause learning to occur but that it can afford certain tasks or experiences that can result learning (Bower, 2008; Dalgarno and Lee, 2010).

Key Ideas In This Book

A number of key ideas that emerged from the VR School Study have been explicated throughout this book. Arguably, some of these ideas are applicable to the practice of and research on embedding emerging technology in schools more generally. In the VR School Study, learning through iVR was approached from multiple perspectives. There was interest in the usual question of whether the technology assisted students with content knowledge acquisition especially when compared to conventional pedagogical approaches. However, learning through iVR was also envisaged as a social activity involving collaborative research, problem-solving, and creativity, a cluster of 'skills' commonly associated with 21st century learning (National Research Council, 2012), and as a means to develop self-directed, metacognitive behaviour (Berk, 2012). This multi-faceted conception of learning influenced the methodological approach used in the study, the way VR experiences were woven through the curriculum, and the choice of 6DOF hardware and 'sandbox' virtual environments that offered content creation tool without the need to learn coding.

Foremost was a consideration of the learning affordances (or specific properties) of the hardware and software that could allow for an embodied sense of interaction, navigation, creativity, verbal and non-verbal communication, and collaboration *within* networked (multi-user) virtual environments. Teachers who are considering the use of emerging technology often ask the question, 'What equipment and/or software should my school invest in?' I would suggest that educators ask more pedagogically valuable questions – What are the learning affordances of iVR applications and how can these be used to create educational opportunities that are not readily accessible or different from those currently available for my students?

This book demonstrates the benefits of asking pedagogical questions through theoretical and empirical insights into how iVR can enrich student learning, curriculum offerings, and the instructional repertoire of the teacher. At its pedagogical heart, this book is not about inanely inciting educators to innovate, as if this were some decontextualised function of an individual educator's inspirational thinking. Instead, I argue that educators should leverage the established instructional strategies of their field and their deep pedagogical knowledge of this, or signature pedagogies (Shulman, 2005), to create immersive learning experiences that resonate with the curriculum and students.

Another important idea arising from the study is that emerging technologies should be carefully incubated in place so that the relationship between the technology and the material realities of different types of educational contexts can be better understood. The common position on evidence of 'What works?' should be reframed in terms of the social realist position of 'What works for whom, in which circumstances and why?' (Nielsen and Miraglia, 2017). As Wong, Greenhalgh, and Pawson (2010) explain:

(N)o deterministic theories can always explain nor predict outcomes in every context. Instead (a realist approach) it is based on the principle that, though human agency and interaction is involved, in certain contexts or situations, individuals are likely, though not always certain, to make similar choices about which resources they will use (so that) … particular contexts influence human choice such that semi-predictable reoccurring patterns of behaviour … occur. (p. 2)

Biesta (2007) argues that the practice of, and by extension research on, pedagogical interventions should not be thought of in a technicised, causal 'input-output' way but as opportunities to understand how students respond to interventions. Incubation of emerging technologies entails bringing together educational practice *with* research to explore and problem-solve in situ in the dynamic setting of the school. This is likely to yield a greater understanding of the various ways students approach the technology especially where there is less than ideal access to hardware and software and teachers are required to design curriculum within material constraints. Importantly, incubation involves reflective practice which allows educators to identify and respond to safety and ethical issues. This is crucial when the technology and/or its applications are profoundly immersive or opaque (for example machine learning applications) in their function or likely to elicit powerful physical, emotional, moral, or social responses related to stages of child development.

This book seeks to highlight the complications and possibilities for using iVR in schools by exploring the intended and unintended effects of embedding the technology into actual classrooms and using methodological approach to capture how students approach learning through the wonders of 'sandbox' virtual environments. The position of this book sits in contrast to the commercial imperative of the EdTech sector to drive the 'scaling up' of immersive technologies. I would suggest that any successful attempt at 'scaling up' immersive technologies will be dependent on developing a much deeper understanding of 'what works' within specific learning contexts and across subject areas of the curriculum and that this will involve 'scaling down' the rhetoric of the EdTech sector to create more substantial, evidence-informed dialogue on the usefulness and limitation of the technology for learning.

Chapter Overview

Readers of this book can dip in and out of chapters of interest; however, to grasp its theoretical threads and conceptual layers it is probably best read in a linear way. The key ideas described above are woven throughout the chapters and responded to through evidence available in the research literature and the presentation of original conceptual frameworks and findings from the VR School Study which sparked ever deeper exploration of the themes of the learning affordances and pedagogies of iVR across the school curriculum.

The journey begins with chapter 2 which provides essential background information. This includes a 'potted' history of iVR and a section on the unique learning affordances or properties of VR that can be of educational benefit (Dalgarno and Lee, 2010), a key idea and analytical tool used in this book. The scholarly literature on the use of the technology in schools is then reviewed. This chapter concludes by addressing child development issues related the ethical and safe use of the technology with children and young people.

The pedagogy of iVR is the focus of chapter 3. Explicit definition and theorising of the pedagogy of iVR is seldom articulated in the literature. This chapter seeks to rectify this by approaching the topic in a theoretically detailed and pragmatic way. To begin, the concept of pedagogy, as it is used in this book, is defined and situated within a broader philosophical purpose of education. The chapter then provides an explanation of levels of theory and their current relationship to educational technology, before going on to review the way the concept of pedagogy is implied or deployed in current iVR literature. In response to gaps identified in the previous section, the chapter then presents an original pragmatic pedagogical framework, the 'Actioned Pedagogy for Immersive Learning' (APIL), and two supporting conceptual models designed to scaffold educators in making sound decisions when choosing, using, and reviewing iVR applications for their classrooms. The first scaffold is a pedagogical typology of iVR designed to help educators think through what an iVR can offer students by the degree of embodied interaction and learner autonomy in an environment. The second scaffold encourages educators to think about iVR in a nuanced way that goes beyond the commonly used 'tech as tool' trope. This includes understanding how iVR application might be used as a form of media, a holistic learning environment with pedagogical assumptions already baked into it or as powerful adjunct experience. This chapter combines a deep dive into theory with original pragmatic and conceptual frameworks designed to provide a more sophisticated approach to understanding the pedagogical potential of IVR.

The book then makes an empirical shift to present a series of chapters on the VR School Study, the first research to embed iVR in secondary school classrooms in a curriculum-aligned way. Chapter 4 describes the methodology for the study, its participatory approach and design, the low-income school settings, instruments, participants, and modes of analysis. Chapter 5 describes the practical and ethical issues associated with embedding highly iVR in high school classrooms with examples of the types of resources and protocols developed to ensure safe implementation. This chapter also provide insights into gender dynamics and engagement with the technology.

Chapter 6 reports on findings from the Callaghan College arm of the research which comprised a mixed method, multi-site investigation of learning through iVR in junior secondary high school science classes. This chapter begins by setting the context, scope, and curriculum approach of the study with a focus on the types of learning outcomes that were investigated. Specifically, the chapter provides an account of three different perspectives on learning that were the foci of the study: (1) content knowledge acquisition; (2) regulation of learning in the networked virtual world of Minecraft VR; and, (3) multiple aspects of the Deeper Learning framework including self-directed learning, communication, collaboration and problem-solving (Noguera, Darling-Hammond, and Friedlaender, 2015). The chapter also includes an analysis of student work samples and qualitative perspectives from students and teachers.

Chapter 7 presents a rich qualitative case study on teaching senior school drama through the 3D iVR art application, Tilt Brush. Set in the rural school community of Dungog High School, the focus of this chapter is on how the teacher leveraged the signature pedagogies of drama teaching to empower students to use Tilt Brush as a virtual design studio to develop their directorial vision for a play they were studying. The chapter draws on student focus groups, video of the students working inside and outside of iVR, and student work samples and brainstorm material to explore the student journey in using the learning affordances to develop sophisticated conceptions of directorial vision realised through symbolic aspects of costume and set design within an immersive environment. Teacher reflections on using iVR for learning conclude the chapter.

The final chapter draws together insights from current research, pedagogical theory, learning science, and the empirical lessons of the VR School Study to grapple with the questions of what we need to know and do to ensure powerful learning through immersive virtual reality in diverse schooling contexts. The chapter outlines what we still need to know to ensure iVR is used for Deeper Learning in schools, followed by a set of propositions on what actions we can take in the arenas of research, initial teacher education, and teacher professional learning so that our knowledge and practice is orientated towards developmentally appropriate, safe, and pedagogically sensible deployment of the technology *across* subject areas of the curriculum.

Through the Portal and Into Immersive Virtual Worlds for Learning

When I first put on the Oculus Rift headset and did the standard training demo which involved interacting with a robot and other virtual wonders in a sci-fi lab, two things happened. The first was that I became so enraptured with the embodied, interactive nature of the experience that I sprained my wrist and didn't feel the injury while I was in VR. The second was a realisation that there was no other technology that could so completely and viscerally transport a student to new universes for learning. Between the safety lesson and the vast pedagogical potential of iVR are a gamut of practical, technical, ethical, and educational considerations that require careful investigation and deliberation if the technology is to be used for powerful learning in schools. My hope is that this book provides an intellectual portal for this type of activity.

References

Berk, L. E. (2012). *Child development*. Boston: Pearson.

Biesta, G. (2007). Why 'what works' won't work: Evidence-based practice and the democratic deficit in educational research. *Educational Theory*, 57(1), 1–22. doi:10.1111/j.1741-5446.2006.00241.x

Bower, M. (2008). Affordance analysis – matching learning tasks with learning technologies. *Educational Media International*, 45(1), 3–15. doi:10.1080/09523980701847115

Dalgarno, B., & Lee, M. J. (2010). What are the learning affordances of 3-D virtual environments?British Journal of Educational Technology, 41(1), 10–32. doi:10.1111/j.1467-8535.2009.01038.x

Google (2019). Degrees of freedom. Retrieved https://developers.google.com/vr/discover/degrees-of-freedom

Gorisse, G., Christmann, O., Amato, E. A., & Richir, S. (2017). First-and third-person perspectives in immersive virtual environments: Presence and performance analysis of embodied users. *Frontiers in Robotics and AI*, 4, 1–12. https://doi.org/10.3389/frobt.2017.00033

Kaptelinin, V., & Nardi, B. (2012). Affordances in HCI: Toward a mediated action perspective. In *Proceedings of the SIGCHI Conference on Human Factors in Computing Systems* (pp. 967–976). New York: ACM. doi:10.1145/2207676.2208541

National Research Council. (2012). *Education for life and work: Developing transferable knowledge and skills in the 21st century*. Committee on Defining Deeper Learning and 21st Century Skills, Division of Behavioral and Social Sciences and Education. Washington, DC: The National Academies Press.

Nielsen, K., & Miraglia, M. (2017). What works for whom in which circumstances? On the need to move beyond the 'what works?' Question in organizational intervention research. *Human Relations*, 70(1), 40–62. doi:10.1177%2F0018726716670226

Noguera, P., Darling-Hammond, L., & Friedlaender, D. (2015). Equal opportunity for deeper learning. Deeper Learning Research Series. Retrieved https://files.eric.ed.gov/fulltext/ED560802.pdf

Rebenitsch, L., & Owen, C. (2016). Review on cybersickness in applications and visual displays. *Virtual Reality*, 20(2), 101–125. doi:10.1007/s10055-016-0285-9

Selwyn, N. (2008) From state-of-the-art to state-of-the-actual? Introduction to a special issue. *Technology, Pedagogy and Education*, 17(2), 83–87, doi:10.1080/14759390802098573

Shulman, L. (2005). Signature pedagogies in the professions. *Daedalus*, 134(3), 52–59. https://www.jstor.org/stable/20027998

Slater, M., & Sanchez-Vives, M. V. (2016). Enhancing our lives with immersive virtual reality. *Frontiers in Robotics and AI*, 3, 1–47. doi:10.3389/frobt.2016.00074

Slater, M., & Wilbur, S. (1997). A framework for immersive virtual environments (FIVE): Speculations on the role of presence in virtual environments. *Presence: Teleoperators & Virtual Environments*, 6(6), 603–616. doi:10.1162/pres.1997.6.6.603

Wong, G., Greenhalgh, T., & Pawson, R. (2010). Internet-based medical education: A realist review of what works, for whom and in what circumstances. *BMC Medical Education*, 10(1), 1–10. doi:10.1186/1472-6920-10-12

2

A BRIEF HISTORY OF VIRTUAL REALITY AND A REVIEW OF RESEARCH ON ITS USE IN SCHOOLS

Introduction

This chapter is arranged into four sections, each contributing essential background information on immersive virtual reality (iVR) and education. The chapter begins with a very brief history of VR which contextualises the current state-of-play of the technology for education. This is followed by an outline of the main conceptual framework for understanding the learning affordances (properties) of VR. Scholarly literature on using iVR for learning in schools is then reviewed. The chapter concludes with a discussion about the ethics of using the technology with children and young people. Where relevant, I have drawn on research about screen-based VR and learning in virtual environments more generally; however, the main focus is on iVR and school education mainly as it relates to scholarly peer reviewed literature published over the last decade. Some reputable web resources are also mentioned. Due to the relatively recent commercial availability of iVR hardware and software, scholarly research on iVR and schooling is still a young field.

A Brief History of Immersive Virtual Reality

Humans have long been interested in creating 3D simulations for leisure, learning, and artistic purposes (Aebersold, 2016; Grau, 2003). One of the earliest 3D technologies, invented in the mid-1800s, was the stereoscope. The stereoscope was a handheld device that allowed people to look through lenses to view a 3D picture formed from a dual (stereo) image. The popular toy known as the View-Master, patented in 1939, also used stereoscopy (The Franklin Institute, 2019). In the 1950s, cinematographer Morton Helig created an arcade-style machine called the Sensorama. While sitting in the Sensorama cabinet a person could view a 3D film with vibration, smell, and stereo sound (Virtual Reality Society, 2019). From the 1960s until the 1980s there were steady developments in computerised flight and military-related simulators (Blascovich and Bailenson, 2011). The term 'virtual reality' was coined by computer scientist Jaron Lanier who, in the 1980s, started one of the first VR companies to sell headsets and haptic gloves (haptic technology simulates a sense of touch) (Lanier, 2017).

During the 1980s and 1990s, VR came alive in literature and popular culture. The cyberpunk literary movement produced tales of dystopian futures in which artificial intelligence and iVR intertwined (William Gibson's novel *Neuromancer* and Neal Stephenson's novel *Snow Crash* are examples of this). 'The Matrix' franchise, with its sombre depiction of unsuspecting humanity trapped in a computer simulation, can be viewed as a cinematic culmination of cyberpunk's fascination with VR. During the 1990s, the gaming industry attempted to commercialise iVR with Sega developing a prototype headset and Nintendo briefly releasing 3D gaming equipment (Ewalt, 2018). This interest in VR is closely related to the evolution of massively multiplayer online gaming in complex virtual worlds mediated via desktop computers or mobile devices, a topic that sits outside of this book but covered elsewhere (Bartle, 2016; Castronova, 2008).

It wasn't until the first two decades of the new millennium that advances in hardware saw a commercial rekindling of interest in iVR. In 2010, Google released stereoscopic 3D Street View and Palmer Luckey created a prototype of the Oculus Rift, a headset with an external tracking system which harnessed high-end computer graphic processing power (Lambo, 2018). In 2014, the very popular and affordable Google Cardboard headset was released with this utilising smart phone technology to create an immersive virtual experience. This was followed by the 2015 launch of the virtual field trip application Google Expeditions which was designed for school children.

In 2016, several companies released expensive, high-end iVR headsets (for example, Oculus Rift and HTC Vive) which worked by being connected by a cord to costly computers with a high quality graphics card (sometimes referred to as 'tethered VR'). In the same year, Sony's PlayStation VR was released for the gaming market. By early 2017, it was estimated that more than two million school children had tried Google Expeditions (Charara, 2017) and in early 2019 Sony announced that retailers had sold 4.2 million PlayStation VR units (Shulman, 2019). In 2018, the first 'all-in-one' or 'stand-alone' VR headsets were released. These headsets did not need to be tethered to a computer or require 'outside-in' positional tracking devices as the headset itself contained the computational power and tracking for high quality VR experiences. By 2019, 'stand-alone' headsets have gone from offering 3DOF to 6DOF experiences.

Today iVR is being used for training purposes in the military, retail, manufacturing, and building industries, and the health sector (Slater and Sanchez-Vives, 2016). Clinical and therapeutic applications are also emerging (Rizzo and Koenig, 2017). iVR is attracting gamers and the social media behemoth

Facebook has made substantial investment in the technology with its CEO Mark Zuckerberg dreaming of one billion people using iVR in the future (ABC News, 2017). Social VR has become a reality, with incredible (seemingly endless) permanent virtual worlds now available for leisure and learning: You can put on a headset and attend conferences and professional meetups; go to church, yoga classes, or the theatre; meet up with strangers and friends to battle monsters on fantasy quests; build your own virtual gardens, home spaces, or sci-fi planets with tools supplied within the platform; or just hang out with people from all over the world.

The potential of iVR for educational purposes and evidence of its efficacy for learning is being explored around the globe. These studies are guided by older theoretical frameworks on understanding the unique affordances (properties/features) of VR for learning, and it is to this literature that we now turn.

The Learning Affordances of Virtual Reality

Since the 1990s, researchers have been developing conceptual frameworks for understanding how the unique features of virtual environments can contribute to learning (Winn, 1993; Youngblut, 1998) with some suggesting that the technology has the potential to transform education (Blascovich and Bailenson, 2011; Hollins and Robbins, 2009). Winn's (1993) early work on desktop computer VR captured the pedagogical potential of the technology beyond procedural learning simulations:

> (I)t is often the case that the power of VR is wasted when it is used for simulation. For example, if you enter a virtual world in which there is a virtual microscope through which you can look at a virtual drop of water, you gain nothing. Learning about the microscopic life-forms that live in the droplet is accomplished far more effectively by using a real microscope in the biology laboratory. The microscope in the virtual world is a transducer (revealing to the eyes what would not otherwise be revealed), and the participant is on the wrong side of it! VR comes into its own when, through a massive change of size, the participant jumps through the virtual microscope's eyepiece and into the drop of water, attaining the same relative size as the microorganisms that live there. At this scale, the experience is first-person. But then you do not need the microscope at all. (p. 11)

Winn's explanation highlights the unique learning affordances of VR, sometimes referred to in the literature as 3D virtual learning environments. The term affordance refers to the actual or perceived properties of something and how these might suggest how it can be used or interacted with (Kaptelinin and Nardi, 2012). The term learning affordance refers to the potential (utility) of a technology for learning (Bower, 2008). Both Dalgarno and Lee (2010) and Mikropoulos and Natsis (2011) sum up the learning affordances of VR as:

1. *First (person) order experiences* that support social constructivist conceptions of learning. For example, seeing the world through the eyes of another or avatar gender body swapping.
2. *Natural semantics* or understanding the basis of something before learning about it in a symbolic or abstract way. For example, manipulating angles before learning about why angles are important in mathematics.
3. *Size and scale manipulation* where users can change the size of themselves, objects, or environments to interact with micro/macro worlds. For example, travelling through the body's artery system as a blood cell.
4. *Reification* or transforming abstract ideas into perceptible representations. For example, understanding the concept of instinct by embodying a fish avatar that must stick with the school in order to maximise survival from predators.
5. *Transduction* or extending user capability to feel 'data' that would normally be beyond the range of their senses or experiences. For example, a simulation of the migration paths of whales that allows the learner to follow the paths of different species around the planet.

Dalgarno and Lee (2010) suggest that affordances of 3D virtual learning environments have the potential to: (1) enhance spatial knowledge; (2) facilitate experiential learning that would otherwise be impossible or impractical in the real world; (3) improve transfer of knowledge and skills learned in virtual environments to real situations; and (4) increase motivation and engagement in learning that could lead to richer collaborations.

De Freitas and Veletsianos (2010) add that 3D virtual learning environments present: (1) new opportunities for creativity in learning through role play and mentoring; (2) open up learning spaces for rehearsal and exploration, experimentation, and user-generated content; and (3) broaden capabilities for learner-led problem-based and exploratory learning.

When Winn (1993) wrote about learning through an embodied VR interaction that made a person feel as though they were swimming with microorganisms, the technical possibility to do this was decades away. This is no longer the case. The arrival of commercially available iVR, with its sophisticated positional tracking and gestural control systems, has heralded renewed interest in simulations and virtual worlds for learning in schools with research on this topic now emerging.

Research on Immersive Virtual Reality and Learning in Schools

There have been several recent reviews focused mainly on screen-based VR and education. In Hew and Cheung's (2010) review of VR in K-12 and higher education, 30% (n=15) of the empirical papers reviewed were on studies conducted in school settings, with most being descriptive in nature. The authors suggest that future research should concentrate on filling gaps in the literature related to: the unique affordances of virtual worlds for learning; providing effect sizes for learning outcomes; and understanding whether student and teacher perceptions of virtual worlds changed over time.

A second review of 53 articles on educational virtual environments found that the majority (40/53) related to science, technology, and mathematics subjects (Mikropoulos and Natsis, 2011). There were only three studies where the learning problem was chosen in collaboration with teachers and only one where the study involved students in a school. The authors found that educators and students had a positive attitude towards VR but that 'technological characteristics like immersion and individual factors like age, gender, computer experience [and] psychological factors affecting presence need to be studied in relation to learning outcomes' (p. 777). They concluded that more research was required on how the features of virtual environments can be pedagogically leveraged for learning. This resonates with Merchant and colleagues' (2014) meta-analysis of the effectiveness of screen-based VR-based instruction on students' learning in K-12 and higher education. This analysis found that game-based learning environments were more effective than virtual worlds or simulations.

A fourth review of the educational potential of 3-D multi-user virtual worlds for Science, Technology, Engineering and Mathematics (STEM) education, predominantly delivered via desktop computers, reported that 17 of the 50 studies published involved school education (Pellas, Kazanidis, Konstantinou, and Georgiou, 2017). The authors found that 3-D multi-user virtual worlds had the potential to engage students in collaborative problem-solving and higher order thinking. They also noted that technical barriers could interfere with learning and that students encountered the challenging task of mastering the features of virtual environments while learning content.

Jensen and Konradsen's (2018) review of 21 experimental studies using head mounted displays (VR headsets) with adult populations noted that the technology is useful for cognitive skills related to remembering and understanding spatial and visual information and affective skills related to the ability to manage emotions in difficult situations. However, they also noted that the cognitive skills that were evaluated in the reviewed research were the lower level skills of remembering or understanding facts and that no research investigated the use of head mounted displays to teach higher level cognitive skills.

Research on iVR in schools is only just emerging. Much of the research, especially on lower cost VR such as Google Cardboard and Expeditions, is descriptive (Craddock, 2018; Vishwanath, Kam, and Kumar, 2017) with research generally outlining implementation of the technology in schools and student and teacher perception of the technology (Chou and Hoisington, 2018; Rodríguez, Morga, and Cangas-Moldes, 2019; Yap, 2016). There is occasional consideration of the impact of the technology on learning through qualitative interviews or focus group data from students (Tudor et al., 2018). The predominance of a descriptive research approach is not surprising given the recent commercial availability of iVR.

There are some studies using high-end iVR in schools. For example, research has been conducted on using dance software to teach middle school aged (predominantly) girls computational thinking and programming in an after-school programme (n=8) (Daily, Leonard, Jorg, Babu, and Gundersen, 2014) and a summer camp (n=16) (Parmar et al., 2016). The same research team undertook an experiment with 36 middle school students (4M, 32F) to investigate how the presence or absence of character customisation influenced learning outcomes (Lin, Parmar, Babu, Leonard, Daily, and Jorg, 2017). The research found that participants with customisable characters had better learning outcomes. Other school-based research, while not using a VR headset but polarised glasses and haptic devices, found that using augmented simulation to learn abstract scientific concepts was associated with a significant effect on achievement (Civelek, Ucar, Ustunel, and Aydn, 2014).

A study involving middle school students in urban and rural settings (n=59) using HTC Vive equipment and Google Earth VR reported high usability and enjoyment of the experience, and that boys had higher self-reported self-efficacy in using the technology than girls (Laine, 2019). The research also found that some children experienced cybersickness and that the teachers considered the technical set-up too complex for integration into everyday classroom use.

A recent study of high school students (n=54) using Oculus Rifts with Minecraft VR in STEM classes found that more attention should be paid to the affective and cognitive responses of students while they are in VR and how these affect attention to task, processing of task-related information, and whether such effects persist as students become more familiar with the technology (Southgate et al., 2019). The study also found that even when students were off-task in VR, most were involved in collaborative activity. This suggested that the embodied sociality of multi-user immersive virtual environments could be harnessed for effective learning.

In summary, research on iVR and learning in schools is nascent. More sustained scholarly attention is required to understand the unique contribution of the technology for learning, how it can be integrated into the curriculum, and the pedagogical underpinnings of effective use in the natural setting of the school classroom. More research is required on how students can use the learning affordances of iVR to master content knowledge, develop higher order thinking, and promote metacognition, problem-solving, and collaboration.

Ethical and Legal Considerations

Researchers has raised serious ethical concerns about exposing children and young people to iVR inclusive of, but beyond, issues of the content of applications. Madary and Metzinger's (2016) code of ethical conduct for using VR issued a timely warning about the possible psychological risks of long term immersion on children. Indeed, there are no large scale longitudinal studies on the effects of immersion on children or adults and this represents a key challenge in assessing risk (Slater, 2014).

Some researchers have suggested that any deployment of iVR with children should be informed by a child development approach (Southgate, Smith, and Scevak, 2017). Child development includes physical (motor and perceptual), cognitive, linguistic, emotional (affective), social, and moral domains, and how these interact together during the broad stages of human development (Berk, 2006). Unlike previous technologies and media, highly iVR can feel extremely real.

For example, Baumgartner and colleagues (2008) highlighted problems with the ability of children to cognitively and affectively regulate iVR experiences. Using an iVR roller coaster ride, they compared prefrontal brain arousal in adults and children (mean age 8.7 years) and found that children were more susceptible to the impact of audio/visual stimuli and were unable to inhibit a sense of presence (feelings of 'being there'). They concluded that there should be more reluctance to 'expose children to emotional virtual reality stimuli as currently practiced' (Baumgartner et al., 2008, p. 11).

In terms of cognitive development, it is important to understand when children distinguish what is real from what is not. Between the ages of three to 12 years, children begin to learn the difference between reality and fantasy (Sharon and Woolley, 2004). There is ample evidence that most young children accept fantastic figures and magical processes as real (Principe and Smith, 2008). Indeed, some experiments have found that when primary (elementary) school children were given an iVR experience some came to believe that it had actually happened (Segovia and Bailenson, 2009; Stanford University Virtual Human Interaction Lab, 2011). This has led some to argue that iVR 'is likely to have powerful effects on children because it can provoke a response to virtual experiences similar to a response to actual experiences' and that when choosing VR content consideration should be given to whether it would be acceptable for the child to have that experience in the real world (Common Sense, 2018, pp. 2–3). At a psychological and philosophical level, exposure to iVR raises questions about the ethics of (unintentionally) implanting false memories in children because of their stage of development makes them unable to distinguish what is real from what is not.

Practically, teachers must apply their knowledge of child development and the individual differences of their learners in relation to the appropriateness of an application's content and the headset manufacturer's health and safety advice to make informed decisions about the safe and ethical use of iVR in their classrooms (Figure 2.1). Southgate, Smith, and Scevak (2017) contend that consideration needs to extend beyond the content of iVR applications to include an assessment of the types of social interaction children at different developmental stages might experience in some types of multi-user virtual environments. This includes consideration of child protection issues. Equipment hygiene procedures should also be implemented.

Manufacturers of VR headsets have released health and safety guidelines, and most have age recommendations. For example, while Google Cardboard has no

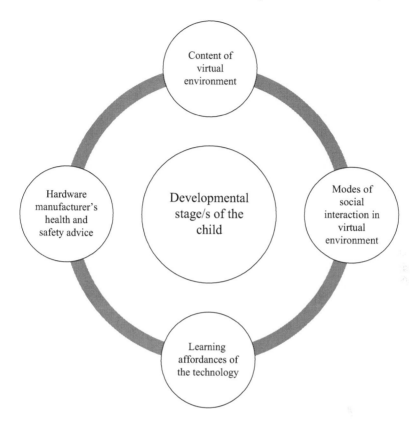

FIGURE 2.1 Conceptual framework for considering aspects of iVR environments within a child development context (adapted from Southgate, Smith, and Scevak, 2017)

age recommendation it is suggested that the equipment be used under adult supervision. Manufacturers of mobile VR (Samsung Gear VR, Google Day-dream), consoles (Sony VR), and high-end VR (HTC Vive, Oculus Rift, Go, and Quest), have age recommendations for use, usually that the child be 13 years or over to use the equipment. Guidelines often stipulate adult supervision and that users take frequent breaks.

One key risk highlighted in manufacturers' guidelines is cybersickness which has symptoms similar to motion sickness (see chapter 1 for more on this). Even though there are engineered solutions to reducing the likelihood of cybersickness, it is difficult to predict if an individual will experience the condition. Much more research, especially related to children and young people, is required in this area to make the use of the technology safer for classroom use.

In the age of harvesting big data and analytics in educational settings (Reidenberg and Schaub, 2018; Rodríguez-Triana, Martínez-Monés, and Villagrá-Sobrino,

2016), it is worth considering the privacy implications of iVR. This includes not only collecting data *about* a person, for example, when they set up an account, but information directly *of* the person, a type of data known as biometrics. Biometric data enables the use of unique physical and behavioural characteristics – such as a person's face, voice or fingerprint, key stroke and gaze patterns and movement – to be used for verification or identification purposes (Royakkers, Timmer, Kool, and van Est, 2018). In iVR, the headset and/or tracking system might be used by manufacturers to collect biometrics data on head, body, arm, and eye movements (Blascovich and Bailenson, 2011). There is even a suggestion that in the near future, pupil dilation will be used as a proxy measure for the affective state or engagement of users (Pan and Hamilton, 2018). The integration of biometric data collection into VR and other immersive technologies represents profound consent and privacy challenges. This is coupled with a lack of transparency regarding if and how this type of data is being collected by manufacturers of iVR equipment and software developers. It is always worth reading the manufacturers' and developers' privacy information in full to ascertain information about biometrics. Furthermore the integration of cameras in some VR headsets and their 'pass through' mode has raised concerns about the ability of technology companies to collect information by filming a user's physical surroundings (Lang, 2019).

There is an increasing likelihood that immersive virtual environments will be infused with artificial intelligence (AI) which will harvest data to make autonomous decisions about what and how students should learn. AI will power pedagogical agents in the form of non-player characters who will help, assess, and direct 'personalised' learning and it will drive more invisible forms of the algorithmic 'nudging' of students towards certain curriculum pathways within virtual environments. To do this, an AI will probably use a combination of biometric and other information about the student supplied by institutions and the student themselves as they use VR educational applications: AI processes this through machine learning algorithms to autonomously determine learning pathways (Southgate, Blackmore, Pieschl, Grimes, McGuire, and Smithers, 2019). While this is a technically and pedagogically complex area, it is worth noting that education has been designated by AI ethicists as a 'high stakes domain' that requires urgent, ongoing scrutiny (Campolo, Sanfilippo, Whittaker, and Crawford, 2017). A coordinated ethical, regulatory, and legislative response is required to ensure that the technology is used for the benefit of students and teachers and that educational products that rely on autonomous decision-making are explainable, transparent, and held to account if harm is done (see Southgate, Blackmore, Pieschl et al. (2019) for a comprehensive ethics, education, and AI framework).

Educators should also be aware of privacy, culturally sensitive images or information, copyright, and intellectual property issues when producing and sharing VR content. This area requires further legal investigation and the development of policy advice for schools. The education sector is attempting to get to grips with the policy, legal, human rights, and ethical implications of using the technology in schools although this is not keeping pace with technical advances (an example of responsible school policy on biometrics is Department of Education (2018)). Given the ethical and legal implications for teachers and students it is important that educators keep apprised of regulation and legislation related to the technology.

Conclusion

This chapter has provided a snapshot of the history of virtual reality and described the learning affordances of the technology. A review of the nascent iVR and schools research literature revealed that the learning benefits of the technology are promising; however much more robust research conducted in diverse school settings is required. Moreover, there are practical, pedagogical, ethical, and legal implications of the technology's use in schools that still need to be addressed.

References

ABC News (2017, October 12). Facebook unveils a VR headset it wants in the homes of one billion users. Retrieved http://www.abc.net.au/news/2017-10-12/facebookma rk-zuckerbergs-vr-gamble/9041904

Aebersold, M. (2016). The history of simulation and its impact on the future. *AACN Advanced Critical Care*, 27(1), 56–61. doi:10.4037/aacnacc2016436

Bartle, R. (2016). *MMOs from the inside out: The history, design, fun and art of massively-multiplayer online role-playing games*. California: Apress.

Baumgartner, T., Speck, D., Wettstein, D., Masnari, O., Beeli, G., & Jäncke, L. (2008). Feeling present in arousing virtual reality worlds: Prefrontal brain regions differentially orchestrate presence experience in adults and children. *Frontiers in Human Neuroscience*, 2, 1–12. doi:10.3389/neuro.09.008.2008

Blascovich, J., & Bailenson, J. (2011). *Infinite reality: Avatars, eternal life, new worlds and the dawn of the virtual revolution*. New York: Harper Collins.

Berk, L. E. (2006). *Child development*. Boston: Pearson.

Bower, M. (2008). Affordance analysis – matching learning tasks with learning technologies. *Educational Media International*, 45(1), 3–15. doi:10.1080/09523980701847115

Campolo, A., Sanfilippo, M., Whittaker, M., & Crawford, K. (2017). *AI now 2017 report*. New York: AI Now Institute. Retrieved https://ainowinstitute.org/AI_Now_2017_Report.pdf

Castronova, E. (2008). *Synthetic worlds: The business and culture of online games*. Chicago: University of Chicago Press.

Charara, S. (2017, May 16). Over two million school kids have gone on Google Expeditions. *Wearable*. Retrieved https://www.wareable.com/vr/expeditions-two-million-ca rdboard-6665

Chou, C. C., & Hoisington, D. A. (2018). Promises and constraints of virtual reality integration: Perceptions from pre-service teachers and K-12 students. In *2018 IEEE 18th International Conference on Advanced Learning Technologies (ICALT)* (pp. 361–363). New York: IEEE. doi:10.1109/ICALT.2018.00098

Civelek, T., Ucar, E.Ustunel, H., & Aydn, M. K. (2014). Effects of a haptic augmented simulation on K-12 students' achievement and their attitudes to-wards physics. *Eurasia*

Journal of Mathematics, Science and Technology Education, 10, 565–574. doi:10.12973/eurasia.2014.1122a

Common Sense. (2018). *Virtual reality 101: What you need to know about kids and VR*. San Francisco: Common Sense. Retrieved https://www.commonsensemedia.org/blog/what-parents-need-to-know-about-virtual-reality

Craddock, I. M. (2018). Immersive virtual reality, Google Expeditions, and English language learning. *Library Technology Reports*, 54(4), 7–10.

Daily, S. B., Leonard, A. E., Jorg, S., Babu, S., & Gundersen, K. (2014). Dancing Alice: Exploring embodied pedagogical strategies for learning computational thinking. In *Proceedings of the 45th ACM Technical Symposium on Computer Science Education SIGCSE '14* (pp. 91–96). New York: ACM. doi:10.1145/2538862.2538917

Dalgarno, B., & Lee, M. J. (2010). What are the learning affordances of 3-D virtual environments? *British Journal of Educational Technology*, 41(1), 10–32. doi:10.1111/j.1467-8535.2009.01038.x

Department of Education (2018). Protection of biometric information of children in schools and colleges: Advice for proprietors, governing bodies, head teachers, principals and school and college staff. Retrieved https://assets.publishing.service.gov.uk/government/uploads/system/uploads/attachment_data/file/692116/Protection_of_Biometric_Information.pdf

De Freitas, S., & Veletsianos, G. (2010). Crossing boundaries: Learning and teaching in virtual worlds. *British Journal of Educational Technology*, 41(1), 3–9. doi:10.1111/j.1467-8535.2009.01045.x

Ewalt, D. (2018). *Defying reality: The inside story of the virtual reality revolution*. New York: Blue Rider Press.

The Franklin Institute (2019) History of virtual reality. Retrieved https://www.fi.edu/virtual-reality/history-of-virtual-reality

Grau, O. (2003). *Virtual art: From illusion to immersion*. Cambridge, Massachusetts: MIT Press.

Hew, K. F., & Cheung, W. S. (2010). Use of three-dimensional (3-D) immersive virtual worlds in K-12 and higher education settings: A review of the research. *British Journal of Educational Technology*, 41(1), 33–55. doi:10.1111/j.1467-8535.2008.00900.x

Hollins, P., & Robbins, S. (2009). The educational affordances of multi user virtual environments. In D. Heider (Ed.), *Living virtually: Researching new worlds* (pp. 257–270). New York: Peter Lang.

Jensen, L., & Konradsen, F. (2018). A review of the use of virtual reality head-mounted displays in education and training. *Education and Information Technologies*, 23(4), 1515–1529. doi:10.1007/s10639-017-9676-0

Kaptelinin, V., & Nardi, B. (2012). Affordances in HCI: toward a mediated action perspective. In *Proceedings of the SIGCHI Conference on Human Factors in Computing Systems* (pp. 967–976). New York: ACM. doi:10.1145/2207676.2208541

Laine, J. (2019). Virtual field trip project: Affordances and user experiences of virtual reality technology in actual school settings. Retrieved https://helda.helsinki.fi/bitstream/handle/10138/300321/Laine_Joakim_Pro_gradu_2019.pdf?sequence=2

Lambo, C. (2018). A brief history of VR. Retrieved https://veer.tv/blog/a-brief-history-of-vr/

Lang, B. (2019, August 6). Here's what Facebook says about camera privacy on Quest & Rift S. Retrieved https://www.roadtovr.com/oculus-quest-camera-privacy-rift-s-facebook/

Lanier, J. (2017). *Dawn of the new everything: A journey through virtual reality*. London: Random House.

Lin, L., Parmar, D., Babu, S. V., Leonard, A. E., Daily, S. B., & Jorg, S. (2017). How character customization affects learning in computational thinking. In *Proceedings of the ACM Symposium on Applied Perception, SAP '17* (pp. 1–8). New York: ACM. doi:10.1145/3119881.3119884

Madary, M., & Metzinger, T. K. (2016). Real virtuality: a code of ethical conduct. Recommendations for good scientific practice and the consumers of VR-technology. *Frontiers in Robotics and AI*, 3, 1–23. doi:10.3389/frobt.2016.00003

Merchant, Z., Goetz, E. T., Cifuentes, L., Keeney-Kennicutt, W., & Davis, T. J. (2014). Effectiveness of virtual reality-based instruction on students' learning outcomes in K-12 and higher education: A meta-analysis. *Computers & Education*, 70, 29–40. doi:10.1016/j.compedu.2013.07.033

Mikropoulos, T. A., & Natsis, A. (2011). Educational virtual environments: A ten-year review of empirical research (1999–2009). *Computers & Education*, 56, 769–780. doi:10.1016/j.compedu.2010.10.020

Pan, X., & Hamilton, A. F. D. C. (2018). Why and how to use virtual reality to study human social interaction: The challenges of exploring a new research landscape. *British Journal of Psychology*, 109(3), 395–417. doi:10.1111/bjop.12290

Parmar, D., Isaac, J., Babu, S. V., D'Souza, N., Leonard, A. E., Jorg, S., Gundersen, K., & Daily, S. B. (2016). Programming moves: Design and evaluation of applying embodied interaction in virtual environments to enhance computational thinking in middle school students. In *Proceedings of 2016 IEEE Virtual Reality (VR)* (pp. 131–140). New York: IEEE. doi:10.1109/VR.2016.7504696

Pellas, N., Kazanidis, I., Konstantinou, N., & Georgiou, G. (2017). Exploring the educational potential of three-dimensional multi-user virtual worlds for STEM education: A mixed-method systematic literature review. *Education and Information Technologies*, 22(5), 2235–2279. doi:10.1007/s10639-016-9537-2

Principe, G. F., & Smith, E. (2008). The tooth, the whole tooth and nothing but the tooth: How belief in the tooth fairy can engender false memories. *Applied Cognitive Psychology*, 22(5), 625–642. doi:10.1002/acp.1402

Reidenberg, J. R., & Schaub, F. (2018). Achieving big data privacy in education. *Theory and Research in Education*, 16(3), 263–279. doi:10.1177%2F1477878518805308

Rizzo, A., & Koenig, S. T. (2017). Is clinical virtual reality ready for primetime? *Neuropsychology*, 31(8), 877–899. doi:10.1037/neu0000405

Rodríguez, J. L., Morga, G., & Cangas-Moldes, D. (2019). Geometry teaching experience in virtual reality with NeoTrie VR. *Psychology, Society, & Education*, 11(3), 355–366. doi:10.25115/psye.v10i1.2270

Rodríguez-Triana, M. J., Martínez-Monés, A., & Villagrá-Sobrino, S. (2016). Learning analytics in a small-scale teacher-led innovations: Ethical and data privacy issues. *Journal of Learning Analytics*, 3(1), 43–65. doi:10.18608/jla.2016.31.4

Royakkers, L., Timmer, J., Kool, L., & van Est, R. (2018). Societal and ethical issues of digitization. *Ethics and Information Technology*, 20(2), 127–142. doi:10.1007/s10676-018-9452-x

Segovia, K., & Bailenson, J. (2009). Virtually true: Children's acquisition of false memories in virtual reality. *Media Psychology*, 12(4), 371–393. doi:10.1080/15213260903287267

Sharon, T., & Woolley, J. D. (2004). Do monsters dream? Young children's understanding of the fantasy/reality distinction. *British Journal of Developmental Psychology*, 22(2), 293–310. doi:10.1348/026151004323044627

Shulman, S. (2019, 25 March). Five Nights at Freddy's, No Man's Sky, and a whole lot more – PS VR owners have a lot to get excited about. Retrieved https://blog.us.playsta

tion.com/2019/03/25/playstation-vr-the-next-wave-of-games-coming-in-spring-a
nd-summer-2019/

Slater, M. (2014). Grand challenges in virtual environments. *Frontiers in Robotics and AI*, 1,
1–4. doi:10.3389/frobt.2014.00003

Slater, M., & Sanchez-Vives, M. V. (2016). Enhancing our lives with immersive virtual
reality. *Frontiers in Robotics and AI*, 3, 1–47. doi:10.3389/frobt.2016.00074

Southgate, E., Smith, S. P., Cividino, C., Saxby, S., Kilham, J., Eather, G., ... & Bergin,
C. (2019). Embedding immersive virtual reality in classrooms: Ethical, organisational
and educational lessons in bridging research and practice. *International Journal of Child-
Computer Interaction*, 19, 19–29. doi:10.1016/j.ijcci.2018.10.002

Southgate, E., Smith, S. P., & Scevak, J. (2017). Asking ethical questions in research using
immersive virtual and augmented reality technologies with children and youth. In *2017
IEEE virtual reality (VR)* (pp. 12–18). New York: IEEE. doi:10.1109/VR.2017.7892226

Southgate, E., Blackmore, K., Pieschl, S., Grimes, S., McGuire, J., & Smithers, K. (2019).
Artificial intelligence and emerging technologies in schools: A research report. Australian Government: Department of Education. Retrieved from https://docs-edu.govcms.gov.au/
node/53008

Stanford University Virtual Human Interaction Lab (2015). Virtual experiences can cause
false memory formation in children. Retrieved https://vhil.stanford.edu/news/2011/
virtual-experiences-can-cause-false-memory-formation-in-children/

Tudor, A. D., Minocha, S., Collins, M., & Tilling, S. (2018). Mobile virtual reality for
environmental education. *Journal of Virtual Studies*, 9(2), 25–36.

Virtual Reality Society (2019). History of virtual reality. Retrieved https://www.vrs.org.
uk/virtual-reality/history.html

Vishwanath, A., Kam, M., & Kumar, N. (2017). Examining low-cost virtual reality for
learning in low-resource environments. In *Proceedings of the 2017 Conference on Designing
Interactive Systems* (pp. 1277–1281). New York: ACM. doi:10.1145/3064663.3064696

Winn, W. (1993). *A conceptual basis for educational applications of virtual reality. Technical publication R-93–9*. Human Interface Technology Laboratory of the Washington Technology Center. Seattle: University of Washington. Retrieved https://cittadinanzadigitale.
wikispaces.com/file/view/1993_winn.pdf/34997779/1993_winn.pdf

Yap, M. (2016). Google cardboard for a K12 social studies module. Retrieved https://
scholarspace.manoa.hawaii.edu/bitstream/10125/40604/1/LTEC-690-Yap-Scholarspa
ce.05.04.16.pdf

Youngblut, C. (1998). *Educational uses of virtual reality technology* (No. IDA-D-2128). Alex-
andria, VA: Institute for Defense Analysis. Retrieved http://papers.cumincad.org/data/
works/att/94ea.content.pdf

3

THE PEDAGOGY OF IMMERSIVE VIRTUAL REALITY

Introduction

This chapter is on pedagogical theory for iVR. The chapter begins by clarifying what is meant by the concept of pedagogy and then proceeds to provide an overview on levels of theory and their relationship to educational technology. These sections establish the foundational definitional, theoretical, and philosophical assumptions about the idea of pedagogy on which this book is based. The chapter then presents a review of the literature on the way the pedagogy of iVR is currently conceived, highlighting applicable gaps. The chapter concludes by presenting an original middle-range pedagogical theory, the Actioned Pedagogy for Immersive Learning (APIL) framework, which is designed to assist educators in making sound decisions in choosing, using, and reviewing iVR applications for their classrooms. The APIL framework is supported by two new scaffolds designed to provide a sophisticated framing of iVR pedagogy which challenge common sense tropes associated with the field. These scaffolds are unpacked in the remainder of the chapter.

What Is Pedagogy?

There is no single definition of pedagogy: It does, however, have a rich vernacular, cross-cultural, and theoretical history (Alexander, 2008; McNamara, 1991). Pedagogy can been defined as the conscious activity of one person designed to enhance learning for another person (Watkins and Mortimore, 1999). In education, there is a divide between pedagogical theories which frame teaching as a set of a generic instructional strategies for the transmission of knowledge across educational settings (sometimes called a *technised* or transmission model of pedagogy) and more philosophically infused theories which consider teaching as a contextualised practice involving the way knowledge is transmitted, exchanged, (co)produced, reproduced, transformed, and challenged. This latter conception views pedagogy as a dynamic practice which is not reducible to a set of a priori instructional techniques for the direct transmission of pre-existing knowledge from teacher to student. It is often linked to a vision of teaching for human flourishing. Lusted (1986) captures the distinction between these two notions of pedagogy when he writes:

> The transmission model (of pedagogy) is unilinear; anyone trying to turn-back in the one-way traffic is unceremoniously run over. To insist on the pedagogy of theory … is to recognise a more transactional model whereby knowledge is produced … in the *consciousness*, through the process of thought, discussion, writing, debate, exchange; in the social and internal, collective and isolated struggle for control of understanding; from engagement in the unfamiliar idea, the difficult formulation pressed at the limit of comprehension or energy; in the meeting of the deeply held with the casually dismissed; in the dramatic moment of realisation that a scarcely regarded concern, an unarticulated desire, the barely assimilated, can come alive, make for a new sense of self, change commitments and activity. And these are also *transformations* which take place across all agencies in an educational process, regardless of their title as … teacher or learner. (p. 4, original emphasis)

It is important in the field education, and especially the sub-field of educational technology, to be precise in the concepts we use, including foundational ideas such as pedagogy. Pedagogy, as understood in this book, is resistant to attempts to 'technise' educative practice (Lingard, 2005). Teaching cannot be reduced to an input-output process where instructional strategies (inputs) are deployed and 'output' accounted for through assessment after learning has occurred (Southgate and Aggleton, 2017). Theoretically, educators can be taught a set of instructional techniques; however, choreographing these through professional judgement for powerful, purposeful learning with diverse group of students and within specific contexts is another matter entirely. Understanding the often unpredictable nature of classrooms and what happens in the 'black box' between input and output is vital if we are to account for effective technology use in education.

Webster (2009) points out that pedagogy is more than a 'means only', it needs to have a clearly explicated end purpose that informs professional judgement. Thus, pedagogy refers to a socially and philosophically infused set of (complicated) intentions and practices that are embedded within the educational traditions, cultures, and institutions in which learning is enacted. As Lusted (1986) explains: 'How one teaches is … of central interest, but through the prism of pedagogy, it becomes inseparable from what is being taught and, crucially, how one learns'.

Thinking pedagogically about emerging technologies such as iVR involves paying close attention to how teachers can leverage their existing pedagogical knowledge and the signature pedagogies of their specialisations to use the learning affordances of virtual environments in curriculum-aligned ways with diverse groups of students. The dynamic interplay between these factors must be set against a well-articulated philosophical position on using the technology for educational purposes – in other words, moving beyond a 'tech as toy or tool' approach to explicitly situate the decision to use iVR within a pedagogical project that purposefully promotes human flourishing for the good of the planet.

The type of thinking and doing skills which reflect this type of philosophical thinking are evident in the 21st century skills approach (National Research Council, 2012) and its related Deeper Learning model (Noguera, Darling-Hammond, and Friedlaender, 2015). The Deeper Learning model focuses on the mastery of academic content in relation to communication and higher order thinking skills. It has six aspects:

1. *Content mastery*: Students acquire knowledge that they then apply or transfer to real world situations. Content mastery is about learning for life.
2. *Effective communication*: Students develop and demonstrate active listening, clear writing, and persuasive presentation.
3. *Critical thinking and problem-solving*: Students consider a variety of approaches to produce innovative solutions.
4. *Collaboration*: Students work with their peers, assume leadership roles, resolve conflicts, and manage projects.
5. *Self-directed learning*: Students use teacher feedback to monitor and direct their own learning, both in and out of the classroom (similar to teaching students regulation skills discussed in chapter 6).
6. *Academic mindset*: Students feel a sense of belonging and the motivation to persist in their school work (Deeper Learning 4 All, 2019).

While the Deeper Learning approach is of benefit to all learners, it was specifically developed to address the equity issues, captured by the deceptively simple term 'the achievement gap', that are a common feature of Western education systems (Noguera, Darling-Hammond, and Friedlaender, 2015). Evaluations show that students from low income schools that use the Deeper Learning approach achieved higher OECD PISA test scores, reported higher levels of collaboration skills, academic engagement, motivation to learn, and self-efficacy, and had better high school graduation and college entry rates than peers at comparison schools that did not implement the model (American Institutes for Research, 2016).

Importantly, Deeper Learning offers a framework for thinking beyond limited 'input-out' conceptions of technology-enhanced learning because it concerns itself with pedagogical dynamics (what happens between input and output) and how the individual and social differences of learners must be addressed in relation to a larger philosophical project of equitable education for a good life. Dede (2014) has suggested that simulation technologies like VR can be powerful means for facilitating Deeper Learning and that more research on this is required:

> [I]mmersive media can be used in a number of ways to promote deeper learning, such as by facilitating case based instruction, collaborative activities, simulated apprenticeships, and the development of scientific inquiry skills, including the collection and analysis of data to provide warrants for specific claims. Simulations allow students to learn skills under controlled conditions that may be difficult to replicate in the real world … but which convey some degree of authenticity, allowing what is learned in one setting to transfer to the other. (p. 18)

The next section of this chapter elaborates on the present state of educational technology theory, arguing that there is a need to develop 'middle-order' pedagogical theory. This type of theory is required so that teachers can better understand how to leverage both the signature pedagogies of their specialisation and the learning affordances of iVR to enable students to develop all the aspects of the Deeper Learning model.

On Theory and Theories of Educational Technology

Education is a multi/interdisciplinary field of research and practice. It has been influenced by: the specialised subject areas that organise set curriculum (derived from the natural, formal, social and applied sciences, humanities, and creative arts); the human-centred disciplines of psychology, sociology, and philosophy which have enabled us to understand learners and learning within and beyond the immediate context of the classroom; and, more specifically, the development of sub-fields of professional knowledge such as curriculum and assessment design, pedagogy, and, more recently, technology-enhanced learning. While the role of theory varies according to each discipline, with each having its own epistemological (knowledge generating) tradition, the multidisciplinary field of education uses educational theory with varying foci and degrees of generalisation.

Sociologists have identified how theory can operate at different levels and be used for a variety of purposes (Giddens, 2009). Theory allows us to: select and frame problems for investigation; draw on and organise knowledge to determine solutions; and formulate predictions and interpret data related to phenomena. There are three levels of theory: (1) universal or generalist theories which seek to predict and generalise explanations about educational, social, and institutional structures, phenomena, and human behaviour (such as learning) across socio-cultural and national contexts, social groups, and time; (2) 'middle-range' theories that are lenses for describing, interpreting, and explaining more concrete and contextualised educational phenomena; and (3) 'micro-range' or localised theories which evolve from and only pertain to practice within very specific educational settings (Higgins and Shirley, 2000). Sociologist Robert Merton (2004/1949) provided the follow explanation of levels of theory and the purpose of middle-range theories:

> [T]heory refers to logically interconnected sets of propositions from which empirical uniformities can be derived. Throughout we focus on what I have called theories of the middle range: theories that lie between the minor but necessary working hypotheses that evolve in abundance during day-to-day research and the all-inclusive systematic efforts to develop a unified theory that will explain all the observed uniformities of social behavior, social organization, and social change. Middle-range theory is principally used in sociology to guide empirical inquiry. It is intermediate to general theories of social systems which are too remote from particular classes of social behavior, organization, and change to account for what is observed and to those detailed orderly descriptions of particulars that are not generalized at all. Middle-range theory involves abstractions, of course, but they are close enough to observed data to be incorporated in propositions that permit empirical testing. Middle-range theories deal with delimited aspects of social phenomena ... (p. 448)

Two of the most popular theories of technology-enhanced learning, the Technological Pedagogical Content Knowledge (TPACK) (Mishra and Koehler, 2006) and the Substitution, Augmentation, Modification, and Redefinition (SAMR) models (Puentedura, 2010) could be characterised as being generalist in their theoretical intent despite being originally rooted in educational practice. TPACK and SAMR are generalist theory because they been developed to be applied across technology types, educational settings (from school to higher education), and the socio-cultural and national contexts of education. Generalist theories are important because they give educators broad thinking tools to design and understand learning through technology.

A potential limitation of a generalist approach is that it does not provide a nuanced enough understanding of how a specific technology can enhance different types of learning for students at diverse developmental stages and in various learning contexts. There is a need to account for such complex dynamics through a finer-grained, middle-range theory that can scaffold educators towards informed decision-making. This is why the APIL framework has been developed. It has an emphasis on the actions educators can take when choosing, using, and reviewing iVR applications. Before presenting APIL, it is beneficial to understand approaches to pedagogy in current literature on iVR.

Conceptions of the Pedagogy in iVR Research

Pedagogy is rarely defined in iVR education research. Instead it is implied or viewed as an adjunct to learning theory. Most often researchers apply, with varying degrees of nuance, learning theories (experiential learning, discovery learning, situated cognition and constructivism) to understand how to design and implement virtual environments for learning (Johnston, Olivas, Steele, Smith, and Bailey, 2018).

The field of immersive learning investigates the conjunction of learning theories and the effects of technical and psychological immersion. This literature explores how immersion can facilitate learning in training stimulations, multi-user virtual environments such as the online games, and specifically designed educational applications. Much of the literature has been about using screen-based VR with university students with some emergent interest in iVR (see contributors to Liu, Dede, Huang, and Richards, 2017). Within the literature, the concept of immersion is treated in two (interrelated) ways. Firstly, it refers to the technical capabilities of a system to approximate movement and interaction in a virtual environment that can evoke feelings of 'presence' or the subjective experience of 'being there' in the environment (Slater and Sanchez-Vives, 2016). Secondly, it denotes psychological immersion where 'mediated, simulated experience … involves the willing suspension of disbelief' (Dede, Jacobson, and Richards, 2017, p. 4). While the focus on immersion is not explicitly pedagogical, it instructional implications are implied as illustrated in Dede et al.'s (2017, pp. 4–5) types of psychological immersion:

1. *Actional immersion*: Empowering users to initiate action or discover new capabilities that can have novel or intriguing consequences.
2. *Symbolic/narrative immersion*: Triggering powerful meanings and associations that can motivate learners or create affective or intellectual connections that can deepen mental models of what is to be learnt.
3. *Sensory immersion*: Immersive displays or headsets can create a panoramic egocentric view of a virtual world or objects that can be harnessed for procedural (knowing how) knowledge or connecting declarative (know what) knowledge with spatial learning.
4. *Social immersion*: Sharing reasoning to get things done and learning along the way with others.

The immersive learning literature has a focus on embodiment. There are technical studies on understanding how to increase a person's senses of body ownership when the real body is substituted for a virtual one with this facilitated through a combination of head mounted display and real time motion-capture tracking (Slater, 2017). Another perspective considers the role of embodying an avatar and their customisation to enhance identity in virtual spaces which in turn can increase a sense of presence and motivation to engage in individual and social activity (Hayes and Johnson, 2019; Lin et al., 2017). The third area explores the notion of implicit learning. This is unconscious learning that may not be able to be explicitly articulated. For example, there is research which indicates that embodying an avatar which has a different ethnicity or gender from oneself can alter biases (Banakou, Hanumanthu, and Slater, 2016). Finally, there is interest in the area of embodied cognition (Wilson, 2002) which involves understanding how learning can be supported in immersive environments through the ways humans interface with machines using their bodies from gestures to full physical movement (Lindgren and Johnson-Glenberg, 2013; Markowitz, Laha, Perone, Pea, and Bailenson, 2018). Overall, the literature on immersive learning suggests that attention should be paid both to cognitive and embodied aspects of learning.

One strand of the immersive learning literature comes from researchers with an affinity for place-based pedagogy, a signature pedagogy (Shulman, 2005) of disciplines which value field trips and placements as part learning. Signature pedagogy refers to favoured ways of teaching in specific disciplines and these are related to the professional practice of the discipline. Klippel and colleagues (2019a, 2019b), from the field of university geoscience, exemplify this approach. Their research concentrates on a taxonomy for immersive virtual field trips to enhance place-based pedagogy. They attempt to explain the influence of the technical specification of VR to create immersion, modes of interaction, and a sense of presence. This research appears promising with university students enjoying immersive virtual field trips more than those experiencing actual ones and exhibiting good laboratory results (Klippel et al., 2019a).

A third, and much rarer, type of pedagogical approach consists of more abstract models that seek to represent the complex relationship between learning outcomes and learner characteristics, the technical aspects of VR simulations and/or virtual worlds (immersion, affordances for action/interaction), and, to a lesser extent, evaluate the influence of instructional strategies within educational contexts (Dalgarno and Lee, 2010; Dengel and Magdefrau, 2018; de Freitas and Oliver, 2006; de Freitas and Veletsianos 2010; Fowler, 2015; Savin-Baden, 2008).

While it is beyond the purview of this chapter to present these generalist theoretical models in full, it is worth highlighting some interesting features. Fowler (2015) building on early work by Dalgarno and Lee (2010) provides a set of frameworks that demonstrate how to design a generic learning specification that could be applied to virtual reality by mapping the relationship between: (1) the broadly defined learning stages of conceptualisation, construction, and dialogue regarding knowledge acquisition; (2) learning outcomes based on Bloom's revised taxonomy of thinking skills (Krathwohl, 2002) which are knowing, remembering, understanding, applying, analysing, evaluating, and creating; and (3) a defined set of learning activities.

Dengel and Magdefrau (2018) present another generalist model designed to illustrate the range of objective and subjective factors which can influence learning in immersive educational environments. Some of these factors are: (1) teacher professional knowledge and practice including instructional type and quality; (2) the technical and psychological potential of immersion to create engagement; and (3) learning activities within and outside of virtual environments. They suggest that their model should be empirically evaluated.

Finally, de Freitas and Oliver (2006) and de Freitas, Rebolledo-Mendez, Liarokapis, Magoulas, and Poulovassilis (2010) offer a middle-range theory for designing and evaluating immersive learning in virtual worlds called 'The Four Dimension Framework'. The first dimension, *learner specifics*, involves profiling the learner and their requirements, aligning learning activities with outcomes, and developing an understanding of how the design of an immersive environment can affect learning and transfer. The second dimension, *pedagogy*, considers the learning and teaching models used in association with virtual environments with the observation that teachers should consider if learning objectives may be met through existing software or if more specifically designed software applications are required. The third dimension, *representation*, asks questions about the degree of interactivity, fidelity, and immersion required for a virtual experience to facilitate learning. The final dimension, *context*, includes whether the learning is taking place in school of informal contexts, the discipline area, and whether the learning is conceptual or applied, the resources available, and the 'hybrid' space of the physical and virtual where learning might occur. One of their most interesting conclusions is that the 'use of immersive learning implies a shift from considering and designing learning tasks to choreographing learning experiences as a whole, mediated by structured and unstructured social interactions' (de Freitas et al., 2010, p. 82).

While most of the models outlined above have emerged from studies of learning related to desktop computer VR, they do illustrate the need to better understand the relationship between the technical, psychological, and social elements of the technology for learning. Less clearly articulated in the literature is: the role of the educator and their pedagogical approach in aligning use of VR with the curriculum and choreographing this in actual classrooms; deploying VR to leverage or expand the potential of signature pedagogies in specific disciplines; and deep, sustained dialogue on the uses of VR beyond a 'means only' teaching tool with elaboration required on how it might be deployed in ways that can accomplish the more philosophical purposes of education for human flourishing.

The use of the generalist theory of constructivism in the immersive learning literature implies a pedagogical approach but rarely explicates what this looks like in practice. Understandably, this literature represents an attempt to interrogate aspects of technical design coupled with an empirical evaluation of content knowledge acquisition, usually through experimental study conducted in controlled lab settings or undergraduate computer science or engineering classes (arguably with students who are already technically minded and able). While it is undeniable that this approach has yielded valuable findings, it reproduces, to varying degrees, a technicist model of education where inputs and outputs are accounted for at the expense of what actually happens between input and output with diverse groups of learners in different settings. Furthermore, it rarely captures the transactional flow of pedagogical dynamics between teacher and learner whereby knowledge is (co)produced. What is required is a middle-range theory that pays more attention to elucidating a non-technicist pedagogy of iVR so that educators can make informed decisions about using the technology with their students. This need provided the impetus towards developing the middle-range APIL framework and its accompanying scaffolds, to which we now turn.

The Actioned Pedagogy for Immersive Learning (APIL) Framework

The APIL framework (Table 3.1) is a middle-range theory which was developed by weaving together insights from learning science and theories of pedagogy, findings from the immersive learning literature, and immediate observation of practice gleaned from our research conducted in schools using iVR (chapters 5, 6, and 7 of this book). The APIL framework is designed to enable educators to take informed action in choosing, using, and reviewing iVR applications within their specific educational contexts and in relation to the developmental and other needs of students.

TABLE 3.1 The Actioned Pedagogy for Immersive Learning (APIL) framework

Teacher realm

1. Clarify why you want to use iVR application instead of another technology/pedagogical approach and identify its learning affordances and how they can assist in meeting learning objectives.
2. Map out how the use of iVR aligns with curriculum objectives, scope, and sequence.
3. Ascertain if the iVR application is being used as an experience, a tool, a form of media for content creation, or a total learning environment.
4. Assess the pedagogical assumptions imbued in iVR applications and consider if these are appropriate for the type of learning you want to enable.
5. Reflect on how iVR can be used to leverage or transform the signature pedagogies used to teach the subject.

Learner realm

6. Ask students how familiar they are with iVR for leisure and learning.
7. Involve students in developing knowledge about the potential risks related to iVR and how to mitigate these.
8. Allow students time to play in iVR so that they can familiarise themselves with hardware, interaction techniques, affordances, and the intensity of experience.
9. Spark students' imagination by guiding their exploration of the learning affordances of an iVR application and explicitly discussing how these can enable learning.
10. Develop integrated activities that provide opportunities for learners to exercise autonomy and develop collaboration, problem-solving, and creative skills inside and outside of iVR. Plan for comparable activities for students who do not like or cannot use iVR.

Technical realm

11. Check manufacturers' health and safety information for hardware and the content appropriateness of software.
12. Consider the developmental stage/s of the learner when choosing hardware and software.
13. Determine spatial, network, and bandwidth requirements for optimal use of hardware and software. Check if the iVR application works in offline mode.
14. In networked (multi-user) applications, consider what appropriate social interaction is and if moderation tools are built into the application.
15. Ascertain if the iVR application has useful, accessible learning analytics.

First and foremost, educators need to critically assess if an iVR experience can provide a unique and powerful way to learn. This involves an examination of the special features of hardware and software to understand how these could be deployed to create educational opportunities that are not readily accessible or different from those currently available. Instead of teachers asking the question 'What specific hardware and software products should I get for my classroom?', the APIL framework prompts educators to systematically work though their technical, pedagogical, and curriculum requirements so that they can assess the suitability of hardware and commercial-off-the-shelf software. APIL is based on a lively, transformational conception of teaching and learning where passive consumption of iVR content may be appropriate on some occasions but not most. Both educator and learner should seek to use the technology to develop but extend beyond content (facts and figures) and procedural knowledge acquisition towards the development of higher order thinking skills (evaluation, analysis, creative processes) and opportunities to practise inter/intra personal skills (self-regulation, communication, collaboration, and problem-solving).

iVR Is Not One Thing: A Scaffolded Approach to Using the APIL Framework

The APIL framework is underpinned by one important assumption — that it is *not pedagogically useful to treat iVR as one thing*. There is a pressing need to go beyond the common trope that putting on a VR headset gives access to one type of 3D world that will automatically prompt learning. A much more nuanced exploration of how the technology can deliver pedagogically different experiences is required. The two scaffolds presented below unpack the key assumption in detail.

Scaffold 1 – Pedagogically, iVR Applications Can Be Classified According to the Degree of Learner Embodied Inter/Action and Autonomy In/With the Learning Experience

iVR is often depicted as though putting on a headset will result in users having one type of pedagogical experience. General definitions of iVR, such as those provided in chapter 1 of this book, are a useful starting point in developing a shared appreciation of the technology's key features and as a way of differentiating it from other immersive technology such as augmented or mixed reality. However, it is not pedagogically useful to consider iVR as a single experiential phenomenon; there is no one type of VR experience. Rather, iVR would be better conceived as a combination of hardware and software enabling or comprising different modes and/or level of embodied interactive experience for learning. There are significant pedagogical implications in coming to grips with this dynamic. Any textual explanation (and one is forthcoming in Table 3.2) needs to be a complemented with embodied, experiential knowledge; that is, by

TABLE 3.2 Typology of iVR environment by learner embodied interaction and autonomy

Type of iVR environments by degree of learner embodied interaction and autonomy	General example	Worked example: learning about reefs
Swivel		
This type of COTS (ready to use) environment relies on a relatively stationary learner, who rotates their head or body (if they are seated on a swivel chair) to experience (see and hear) the surrounding virtual world that might be a fully computer generated simulated experience or a 360° photograph or video. This type of VR is usually experienced individually although some multi-user applications are available.	Develop an understanding of life in a rainforest, through sight and sound, by remaining relatively stationary and looking around from a tree branch and seeing flora and fauna. Being seated beside a famous monument and looking up at it and taking in how it is situated in the surrounding landscape.	Existing 360° video experience or VR app allows the seated learner to look around and see fish and other sea life in the reef swimming amongst coral. Teacher uses this as stimulus media in a lesson to spark engagement and start a learning activity.
Explore		
This type of COTS environment allows for unguided or guided exploration and navigation either through a hand-held controller or gaze (looking at predetermined areas highlighted in the environment) to explore fully simulated or adjoining 360° photograph/video environments which may have annotations, video, pictures, and animations embedded in them. In some cases it may be possible to interact with elements or non-player characters in the environment using a controller, voice, or gaze e.g. embedded multi-media pops up within the environment at certain stages or when interacted with. It can be experienced individually or with others depending on technical features and design.	A simulation of a real museum where the learner can navigate through gallery rooms and be presented with information in different media forms about artefacts. A tour of a prehistoric landscape with a bird that swoops down at a specific point to describe the ancient ecosystem.	A tour application which allows the class to go on an expedition to a reef together and where students are guided by the teacher or a non-player character to learn about key features which are annotated or animated with information.

(Continued)

TABLE 3.2 (Cont.)

Type of iVR environments by degree of learner embodied interaction and autonomy	General example	Worked example: learning about reefs
Discover		
A virtual environment with fully interactive activities and tools to enable learners to undertake self-directed learning that is fully curriculum or competency aligned. Can include training scenario or inquiry/discovery-based learning, undertaken individually or in groups. Could include ongoing, personalised feedback and/or pathways through learning activities.	A virtual laboratory is equipped to do the types of experiments that can be conducted in an actual lab but with no real world safety issues to be concerned about. A simulation of the human body where the learner can travel in microscopic mode at their own pace through biological systems of choice to collect data in order to understanding the structure and function of a biological system or diagnose a medical condition.	A multi-user virtual world that has been specifically designed for learners to 'swim' about in reef ecosystem. The virtual world allows learners to explore the reef in groups at their own pace. Learners can manipulate elements such as ocean temperature and view the results on the reef ecosystem before their eyes. They can record observational data (e.g. coral bleaching zones) and other information to solve puzzles about ocean life which act as a formative assessment.
No code create		
Sometimes referred to as sandbox virtual environments, the learner is supplied with an authoring or content creation toolbox which allows them to create their own 3D maps, models, designs, prototypes, and art work without needing to code. These can be individual or multi-user collaborative environments. Teachers can have students use the content creation tools to illustrate content mastery through imaginative learning tasks.	A virtual environment provides the learner with the tools to recreate the built and natural landscape of an historical battle with annotated information provided at different points about the event as users move through it. Learners collaborate in VR to prototype a full size set design for the school play experimenting with scale, allowing for virtual blocking for actors, and providing different versions of lighting and sound effects to inform the building of the real life theatre set. Classmates and the teacher go into the environment to provide feedback at each design phase.	A networked sandbox application is identified which gives students the tools to visibly translate their research/content mastery on a self-directed topic of interest on reefs by manipulating size/scale in VR e.g. to show how different parts of a reef are experienced from the perspective of a seahorse. Students work in groups to research this topic and decide how best to include information and design the experience for other learners who evaluate it through a peer assessment process.

Code-to-create

This involves the learner using game engines or similar (e.g. Unity, Unreal Engine) that require coding to create virtual worlds from the beginning of the process (it can also involve using existing 3D assets/models for inclusion in the project and designing interfaces for human interaction and user experience). Because this involves a high degree of coding and technical mastery, this approach is usually located in computer science or ICT classes where the objective is to have learners mature their programming knowledge in the same way a developer will apply programming/design thinking skills to create a VR product.

Learners use a game engine to meet learning outcomes related to programming and design thinking by creating a virtual environment for other students e.g. recreating what a World War I trench was like for peers who are studying History.

In a computer science class, students work in groups in a lab to use a game engine to create a reef with interactive components which demonstrate mastery of content knowledge about reefs, design thinking, and programming skills. Peers who are studying reefs as part of Geography provide usability feedback on the design.

Social VR

Social VR consists of commercial (but mostly free to join) permanent 3D virtual worlds that allows people with VR equipment (and sometimes in 2D mode) to socialise, play games, and meet for leisure and learning. Some sites allow users to create public or private events and may provide content creation tools for users to make or customise their own environments. Most social VR platforms are not appropriate for children under the age of 13, unless there is a junior mode. Only some social VR is moderated and so consideration of child protection issues is paramount.

Learners from all over the world meet up as avatars to attend a virtual conference or practise a skill such as learning a second language with native speakers or gather to watch a concert or a play staged in VR.

Students attend a virtual lecture from a leading expert on the environmental management of reefs and are able to interact with the expert in real time.

educators trying out, experimenting, and playing with different types of hardware and diverse iVR applications which allow for many and varied interaction techniques. As an experiential technology, educators must learn about immersive learning by playing with/in different types of iVR technology.

Different types of iVR offer design features that allow people to interact with and even create their own virtual objects and worlds. Some techniques include: gaze-based interaction where the user can manipulate objects and move around by directing where they look in the environment; ray-casting which is a point-and-pick technique; and 6DoF gestural interaction which relies on special controllers that provide virtual hands; and various other modes for navigating and moving around horizontally, vertically, and diagonally through a smooth motion, teleporting (jumping from spot to spot), or clicking on portals. Add to this the ability to interact with other people in networked (multi-user) virtual environments and the diversity of iVR experiences increases. The technical aspects of iVR environments create very different experiences and possibilities for learner autonomy beyond the content domain. Hence, the assertion that pedagogically iVR should not be considered as one thing.

In technical discussions about iVR there is often a dichotomy established between passive and active experiences and between 360° media and fully realised 3D virtual environments or worlds. This type of categorisation is limiting because it does address pedagogical potential. For example, a 'passive' virtual experience can be used as a powerful stimulus for an engaging lesson. Similarly, there have been frequent technical discussion on excluding 360° media from the iVR category even though they can be experienced using a headset. The argument goes that legitimate iVR should only be conceived as a fully realised, spatially developed, interactive 3D environment. As Table 3.2 illustrates, this distinction is not pedagogically useful as some 360° platforms provide students with the opportunity to create media rich immersive environments with interactive hotspots that can be used to add photographs, videos, text, or animations to tell a story. Portals can connect 360° photography or video environments together to create an opportunity to develop non-linear, branching narratives. This type of 'sandbox' platform provides the tools for students to create sophisticated, interactive immersive worlds without needing to code and so are not pedagogically inferior to more fully realised 3D computer generated environments. Any pedagogical model needs to account for learning with the technology not just in the technology. Indeed, if the learning outcomes involves creativity, communication, and problem-solving skills, as well as mastery of multi-media content creation both for the foundation environment and for pop-up content, then a 360° platform could enable higher order thinking (Krathwohl, 2002) and Deeper Learning (Noguera, Darling-Hammond, and Friedlaender, 2015) in ways that a poorly designed interactive 3D virtual world might not. Furthermore, given the reported issue of some younger children developing false memory from iVR environments, it may be that the less immersive experiences of 360° media are more developmentally appropriate for younger students.

Table 3.2 is a non-hierarchical typology which classifies different types of iVR by the manifestation of and intersection between the following characteristics:

1. Degree of embodiment or what you can do with your real and avatar's body in the virtual environment.
2. Potential to have an effect (interact with, navigate, create within) on the virtual environment or objects or agents (avatars and non-player characters) in it in some meaningful way.
3. Extent of autonomy over learning in/with the virtual environment.

The typology includes a worked example to illustrate each an idealised type of iVR in relation to education. Like all typologies it reduces complexity and does not capture hybrid forms; however, its nuanced classificatory properties coupled with practical illustrations mark a conceptual and explanatory improvement on the simplistic passive-active classificatory dichotomy that currently exists.

Scaffold 2: There Is a Need to Move Beyond the 'Tech as Tool' Metaphor

How can educators think about iVR in relation to curriculum? Is it a learning experience, a form of digital media, an instructional tool, or an environment that supplies tools with experiences for learning, or a total learning environment that allows students to return to deepen their learning (Figure 3.1)? VR can be conceived of as any or all of these things depending on its design, affordances for learning, and how it is used in the classroom. As the Scaffold 1 typology (Table 3.2) demonstrates, immersive environments range from swivel 360° photography and video to vast 3D computer generated multi-user simulated worlds where anything seems possible.

Pedagogically, the power of immersive environments is not necessarily tied to their interactive sophistication, access to content creation tools, or even the 'realness' (fidelity) of the experience. Rather, it is in the educator creatively considering how the technology aligns with learning objectives and their philosophy of the purpose of education. For example, a 'swivel' experience such as a 360° video while relatively passive in terms of embodied interaction can be a powerful learning experience if its content and visual narrative are carefully crafted for affective and cognitive impact. An educator needs to exercise professional judgement on where such an experience might best fit in to the curriculum as a stimulus material for a lesson or as a supplementary media for enriching understanding. Alternatively, a science educator may choose to use an all-in-one interactive total learning environment, such as a 3D virtual laboratory, because real life facilities may not be available or because the application can easily offer something the real world cannot, the ability to conduct variations on an

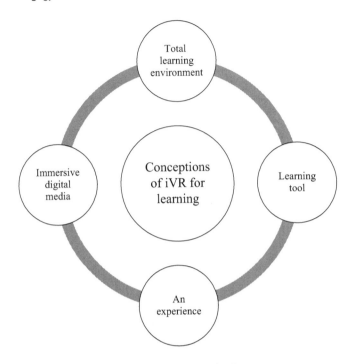

FIGURE 3.1 Conceptions of the pedagogical uses of iVR

experiment without wasting resources. Moreover, using a total learning environment such as a virtual lab is an easier fit with science as it leverages off a signature pedagogy of the discipline which is lab work and this aligns with the learning objectives of mastering the skills of experimentation.

Some iVR environments, in particular those based on sandbox design principles, provide content creation (authoring) tools to use in a studio environment. This allows educators to devise creative learning tasks for students to demonstrate knowledge mastery and/or ability to collaborate, communicate, or problem solve. For example, using the networked (multi-user) environment of Minecraft VR as part of drama lessons students could work together in the world to build the setting for Shakespeare's play *Romeo and Juliet*, the historical town of Verona, with their avatars acting out scenes in-situ with peers acting as the audience. Some iVR applications are designed as virtual simulation tools for procedural training, for example learning a resuscitation procedure on a virtual human with feedback delivered in an ongoing manner as the user practises their technique.

iVR, and digital technologies generally, are often framed as teaching and learning 'tools'. The 'tool' metaphor persists because it empowers educators to think about using technology for specific purposes rather than assuming the technology will automatically facilitate learning. The 'tool' metaphor is often accompanied by the mantra 'pedagogy before technology', which is also designed to prompt educators to think about why they are using a particular technology for learning. The case of VR for education presents some challenges to these common sense approaches. Firstly, as demonstrated above, iVR can provide tools to deepen understanding, act as a form of media for content creation, or offer a unique one-off experience; however, in some cases iVR can be a total learning environment in which a range of interconnected learning activities has been scoped and sequenced in relation to a set of lesson plans that may or may not include out-of-VR learning activities. Some total iVR environments have the pedagogical principles and instructional strategies infused into them including forms of assessment. This type of iVR learning environment is already under-pinned by a pedagogical vision of what knowledge and skills the learner should master and at what level of competency, and usually includes a teacher guide or set of lesson plans to follow. Even iVR applications that can be used as discrete learning experiences, such as virtual field trips, are imbued with pedagogical intent: They are created with a particular vision of the learner and what learning is even if, in some cases, this is not overtly explicated or adequately informed by educational theory. Such iVR applications should not be conceived as neutral learning tools.

This is not to say that educators cannot use iVR applications in ways contrary to the pedagogical intent that has been 'baked' into them. Rather, it is to high-light the need for educators to critically evaluate the pedagogical underpinnings of iVR applications in order to critically assess if these complement learning objectives and satisfy broader philosophical purposes of education. This last point is particularly pertinent as it requires reflection on the use of iVR applications to develop aspects of Deeper Learning (Noguera, Darling-Hammond, and Frie-dlaender, 2015) and higher order thinking (Krathwohl, 2002).

Conclusion

This chapter has outlined the idea of pedagogy as a non-technised transforma-tive and negotiated practice and argued that this conception should inform the development of a middle-range theory for the pedagogy of iVR that can sup-port educators to facilitate Deeper Learning and higher order thinking with their students. The chapter scoped out current pedagogical perspectives in the immersive learning literature, highlighting the need to create the new APIL pedagogical framework for iVR and education. APIL is underpinned by two scaffolds designed to increase educators' understanding of types of iVR and their varied potential uses in education. There is an urgent need to develop our pedagogical understanding of the technology beyond simplistic dichotomies such as 'passive' and 'active' or the 'tech as tool' metaphor to encompass a more sophisticated conceptions of choreographing learning (de Freitas et al., 2010) through iVR. This is vital if the pedagogical potential of the technology is to be fully realised.

References

Alexander, R. (2008). *Essays on pedagogy*. London and New York: Routledge.

American Institutes for Research (2016). Does deeper learning improve student outcomes? Results from the study of deeper learning: Opportunities and outcomes. Retrieved https://www.air.org/sites/default/files/Deeper-Learning-Summary-Updated-August-2016.pdf

Banakou, D., Hanumanthu, P. D., & Slater, M. (2016). Virtual embodiment of white people in a black virtual body leads to a sustained reduction in their implicit racial bias. *Frontiers in Human Neuroscience*, 10, 1–12. doi:10.3389/fnhum.2016.00601

Dalgarno, B., & Lee, M. J. (2010). What are the learning affordances of 3-D virtual environments? *British Journal of Educational Technology*, 41(1), 10–32. https://doi.org/10.1111/j.1467-8535.2009.01038.x

Dede, C. (2014). The role of digital technologies in deeper learning. Students at the center. Retrieved https://files.eric.ed.gov/fulltext/ED561254.pdf

Dede, C., Jacobson, J., & Richards, J. (2017). Introduction: virtual, augmented, and mixed realities in education. In D. Liu, C. Dede, R. Huang, & J. Richards (Eds.), *Virtual, augmented, and mixed realities in education* (pp. 1–16). Singapore: Springer.

Deeper Learning 4 All (2019) What skills should students have? Retrieved from https://deeperlearning4all.org/

De Freitas, S., & Oliver, M. (2006). How can exploratory learning with games and simulations within the curriculum be most effectively evaluated? *Computers & Education*, 46 (3), 249–264doi:10.1016/j.compedu.2005.11.007

De Freitas, S., & Veletsianos, G. (2010). Crossing boundaries: Learning and teaching in virtual worlds. *British Journal of Educational Technology*, 41(1), 3–9. doi:10.1111/j.1467-8535.2009.01045.x

De Freitas, S., Rebolledo-Mendez, G., Liarokapis, F., Magoulas, G., & Poulovassilis, A. (2010). Learning as immersive experiences: Using the four-dimensional framework for designing and evaluating immersive learning experiences in a virtual world. *British Journal of Educational Technology*, 41(1), 69–85. doi:10.1111/j.1467-8535.2009.01024.x

Dengel, A., & Mägdefrau, J. (2018). Immersive learning explored: Subjective and objective factors influencing learning outcomes in immersive educational virtual environments. In *2018 IEEE International Conference on Teaching, Assessment, and Learning for Engineering (TALE)* (pp. 608–615). New York: IEEE. doi:10.1109/TALE.2018.8615281

Fowler, C. (2015). Virtual reality and learning: Where is the pedagogy? *British Journal of Educational Technology*, 46(2), 412–422. doi:10.1111/bjet.12135

Giddens, A. (2009). *Sociology*. Cambridge: Polity Press.

Hayes, A., & Johnson, K. (2019). Cultural embodiment in virtual reality education and training: A reflection on representation of diversity. In M. Chang, E. Popescu, Kinshuk, N-S. Chen, M.Jemni, R.Huang, J. M.Spector, and D. G. Sampson (Eds.), *Foundations and Trends in Smart Learning* (pp. 93–96). Singapore: Springer. doi:10.1007/978-981-13-6908-7_13

Higgins, P. A., & Shirley, M. M. (2000). Levels of theoretical thinking in nursing. *Nursing Outlook*, 48(4), 179–183. doi:10.1067/mno.2000.105248

Johnston, E., Olivas, G., Steele, P., Smith, C., & Bailey, L. (2018). Exploring pedagogical foundations of existing virtual reality educational applications: A content analysis study. *Journal of Educational Technology Systems*, 46(4), 414–439. doi:10.1177%2F0047239517745560

Klippel, A., Zhao, J., Jackson, K. L., LaFemina, P., Stubbs, C., Oprean, D., Wallgrün, J. O., & Blair, J. (2019a). Transforming earth science education through immersive experiences - delivering on a long held promise. *Journal of Educational Computing Research*, 57(7), 1745–1771. doi:10.1177%2F0735633119854025

Klippel, A., Zhao, J., Oprean, D., Wallgrün, J. O., & Chang, J. S. K. (2019b). Research framework for immersive virtual field trips. In *2019 IEEE Conference on Virtual Reality and 3D User Interfaces (VR)* (pp. 1612–1617). New York: IEEE. doi:10.1109/VR.2019.8798153

Krathwohl, D. R. (2002). A revision of Bloom's taxonomy: An overview. *Theory into Practice*, 41(4), 212–218. https://doi.org/10.1207/s15430421tip4104_2

Lin, L., Parmar, D., Babu, S. V., Leonard, A. E., Daily, S. B., & Jörg, S. (2017). How character customization affects learning in computational thinking. In *Proceedings of SAP* (pp. 1–8). Cottbus, Germany, September 16–17. doi:10.1145/3119881.3119884

Lingard, B. (2005). Socially just pedagogies in changing times. *International Studies in Sociology of Education*, 15(2), 165–186. https://doi.org/10.1080/09620210500200138

Lindgren, R., & Johnson-Glenberg, M. (2013). Emboldened by embodiment: Six precepts for research on embodied learning and mixed reality. *Educational Researcher*, 42(8), 445–452. doi:10.3102%2F0013189X13511661

Liu, D., Dede, C., Huang, R., & Richards, J. (Eds.) (2017). *Virtual, augmented, and mixed realities in education*. Singapore: Springer.

Lusted, D. (1986). Why pedagogy? *Screen*, 27(5), 2–16. doi:10.1093/screen/27.5.2

Markowitz, D. M., Laha, R., Perone, B. P., Pea, R. D., & Bailenson, J. N. (2018). Immersive virtual reality field trips facilitate learning about climate change. *Frontiers in Psychology*, 9, 1–20. doi:10.3389/fpsyg.2018.02364

McNamara, D. (1991). Vernacular pedagogy. *British Journal of Educational Studies*, 39(3), 297–310. https://doi.org/10. 1080/0007 1005. 1991. 9973 892

Merton, R. (2004/1949). On sociological theories of the middle range. In Calhoun, C., Gerteis, J., Moody, J., Pfaff, S., & Virk, I. (Eds.), *Classical sociological theory* (pp. 448–459). London: John Wiley & Sons.

Mishra, P., & Koehler, M. J. (2006). Technological pedagogical content knowledge: A framework for teacher knowledge. *Teachers College Record*, 108(6), 1017–1054. doi:10.1111/j.1467-9620.2006.00684.x

National Research Council. (2012). *Education for life and work: Developing transferable knowledge and skills in the 21st Century*. Committee on Defining Deeper Learning and 21st Century Skills, Division of Behavioral and Social Sciences and Education. Washington, DC: The National Academies Press.

Noguera, P., Darling-Hammond, L., & Friedlaender, D. (2015). Equal opportunity for Deeper Learning. Jobs for the future. Retrieved https://files.eric.ed.gov/fulltext/ED560802.pdf

Puentedura, R. (2010). SAMR and TPCK: Intro to advanced practice. Retrieved http://hippasus.com/resources/sweden2010/SAMR_TPCK_IntroToAdvancedPractice.pdf

Savin-Baden, M. (2008). From cognitive capability to social reform? Shifting perceptions of learning in immersive virtual worlds. *ALT-J*, 16(3), 151–161. doi:10.1080/09687760802526731

Shulman, L. (2005). Signature pedagogies in the professions. *Daedalus*, 134(3), 52–59. https://www.jstor.org/stable/20027998

Slater, M. (2017). Implicit learning through embodiment in immersive virtual reality. In D. Liu, C. Dede, R. Huang, & J. Richards (Eds.), *Virtual, augmented, and mixed realities in education* (pp. 19–33). Singapore: Springer.

Slater, M., & Sanchez-Vives, M. V. (2016). Enhancing our lives with immersive virtual reality. *Frontiers in Robotics and AI*, 3, 1–47. doi:10.3389/frobt.2016.00074

Southgate, E., & Aggleton, P. (2017). Peer education: From enduring problematics to pedagogical potential. *Health Education Journal*, 76(1): 3–14. doi:10.1177%2F0017896916641459

Watkins, C., & Mortimore, P. (1999). Pedagogy: What do we know? In P. Mortimore (Ed.), *Understanding pedagogy and its impact on learning* (pp. 1–19). London: Sage.

Webster, R. S. (2009). Why educators should bring an end to pedagogy. *Australian Journal of Teacher Education*, 34(1), 42–53.

Wilson, M. (2002). Six views of embodied cognition. *Psychonomic Bulletin & Review*, 9(4), 625–636. doi:10.3758/BF03196322

4

THE METHODOLOGY OF THE VR SCHOOL STUDY

This section of the book, encompassing chapters 4, 5, 6, and 7, reports on findings from the VR School Study, a multi-site investigation that aimed to understand how to embed highly iVR in the school classrooms for Deeper Learning. The VR School Study provided the first substantive research on the use of iVR in the natural setting of the high school classroom and as an extension of curriculum and teacher pedagogy (Southgate et al. 2019). In this chapter, the context for and methodological approach to the study is described in relation to the school communities in which the research was conducted.

Study Setting and Approach

Callaghan College

The VR School Study began as a collaboration between the University of Newcastle and Callaghan College, Australia. Callaghan College has three campuses – one senior and two junior high schools. It has a Future Learning Team that oversee strategic digital initiatives across campuses. The two junior high schools participated in the study with the college principal and teachers from the Future Learning Team involved as co-researchers. The two junior high schools serve students from Years 7–10 (12–16 years old). One junior high school is located in an inner suburban area (740 student enrolments), while the other is outer suburban (1000 student enrolments). Callaghan College is a low-income school community, with the junior high schools having between 44%–48% of students from the lowest socioeconomic status (SES) quartile. While 2.3% of Australia's population identify as Indigenous, 12%–15% of students at the schools are Indigenous. Research based on Australian standardised test scores indicate that, in general, there is a persistent and significant gap of between 2–3 years in literacy and numeracy achievement between high SES students and those from low SES and Indigenous backgrounds (Cobbold, 2017). In the context of their students' economic hardship, Callaghan College pursued a focus on technology-enhanced learning to maximise student learning outcomes and life opportunities. The study at Callaghan College focused on the use of iVR in STEM classrooms, specifically science and information and communication technology (ICT) elective classes. The research began without funding. Eventually, the college attracted a $50,000 grant from the Australian Government's Digital Literacy School Grants Scheme. Most of this funding went towards the purchase of VR and computing equipment and paying for substitute staff to free up time for teachers to develop the study. The study was conducted in two phases spanning 2016–2018.

Dungog High School

The other school to participate in the VR School Study was Dungog High School, located one hour north-west of Newcastle in dairy and timber country. The rural town of Dungog and its surrounds has a population of around 2000 people. Dungog High School has 620 students in Years 7–12 with 50% of these from the lowest SES quartile and 12% from Indigenous backgrounds. As a rural comprehensive high school, it offered traditional academic subjects, creative arts, and vocational courses with a co-curricular programme that included choir, cattle judging, debating, and sports coaching. The VR school team at Dungog High School comprised the head teacher of Creative and Performing Arts (CAPA), the eLearning coordinator, and the librarian. The study at Dungog High School focused on using highly iVR with a senior drama class in 2018. The school funded the purchase of equipment and provided time for the head teacher to work on the project. This represented a significant investment in the project for a rural school in a low-income community.

Approach

The VR School Study was participatory research. This is a form of inquiry that involves collaboration to enable people to investigate aspects of their lives, including work and education, so that they can be empowered to make change for the better (Kemmis and McTaggart, 2008). This was research *with* teachers and students not on them and was premised on the belief that teachers should be part of building the evidence base for their profession. The research team consisted of the university researcher and teachers from the schools. The research had no precedent to draw on to address the ethical, safety, practical, and pedagogical aspects associated with embedding high-end iVR in real school classrooms. The research teams in each school community made collective decisions on the study's participants (which classes would be involved), what classroom arrangements needed to be made to accommodate the spatial requirements of highly iVR, and how the study would fit within complicated school timetables. Each research team collaboratively developed the aims, research questions, and methodological approach for their respective study.

Aim, Research Questions, and Institutional Ethics

The study aimed to explore how highly iVR could be ethically embedded in the natural setting of high school classrooms to promote deep learning. It was guided by the following research questions:

1. What happens when students and teachers use iVR for learning?
2. How can the curriculum be tailored to use the affordances of iVR and how can we assess if it enhances learning, including collaboration?
3. What are the opportunities and challenges of using the latest iVR technology in low-income school communities?
4. How do students and teachers experience iVR in their classrooms?
5. Given the developmental stages of learners, how can we use this type of technology safely and ethically in schools?

The VR School Study was approved by the University of Newcastle Human Ethics Committee (Approval No. H-2017–0229) and the New South Wales Department of Education (Approval No. 2017396). Students at Callaghan College and Dungog High School received a study invitation pack comprising an information statement, parent/guardian consent and child assent form, and a health and safety screening survey. The study information statement had a photo of a student wearing an Oculus Rift headset and was written in plain English text. A video information statement was also recorded and put on the project website for parents/guardians and students who might have lower literacy proficiency. The information statement and associated consent/assent form provided for public sharing of photographs and video from the study for research purposes provided the faces of students were obscured. No individual students are identified in reporting of findings from the study with pseudonyms or generic descriptors (student 1, student 2 etc.) used in attributing quotes from qualitative data.

Methodology, Participants, and Data Scope

Callaghan College

The research conducted at Callaghan College and Dungog High School produced rich case studies on embedding iVR within the natural setting of the school classroom. The Callaghan College research used a mixed method design conducted in two phases. In all, 102 students (46F, 61M) aged 13–16 years participated in VR classes. Phase 1, conducted in November–December 2017, concentrated on the considerable endeavour of solving technical, safety, and pedagogical challenges – of trialling the hardware and software, developing educational resources and protocols to mitigate risk, and allowing the students and teachers time to play with the learning affordances of iVR (see Southgate et al., 2018). This phase collected qualitative data in the form of: student work samples inside of iVR; student and teacher written reflections; audio and video interviews with students and teachers; and handheld and screen capture video of the students working in VR (Table 4.1). Fifty-four students participated in phase 1 of the study. They were from two Year 8 sciences classes (aged 13–14 years) and a Year 9 ICT elective class (aged 14–15 years). Forty-one per cent were female. The safety and ethical resources and protocols developed during phase 1 of the research are discussed in chapter 5 with findings related to learning outcomes from phase 2 of the research reported in chapter 6.

Phase 2 of the research conducted in June–August 2018 investigated using iVR to enhance learning outcomes aligned with the science curriculum. Forty-eight (21F, 27M) Year 9 students, aged 13–15 years from two mixed-ability science classes, participated in the VR component of the study. Phase 2 used a mixed methodology with a quasi-experimental design component. This pre- and post-knowledge test comprised 30 identical multiple choice questions on facts and concepts from the unit of work. It was devised by the teachers and administered through the learning management system. This component had a VR group

TABLE 4.1 Type and scope of data for Callaghan College research

Type of data	Phase 1	Phase 2
In-class observational hours	25h 30m	38h
Audio recording in VR room	22h 48m	15h 50m
Handheld video recording	5h 39m	3h 26m
Screen capture	18h 9m	21h 1m
In-class student interviews	17 interview (31% of participants): 21 boys (5 in ICT and 16 in science) and 8 girls. Length range 20s – 5m.	35 interview participants (73% of sample, 16F, 19M). Length range 20s – 12m.
Researcher reflection	8222 words (university researcher) and 900 words (teacher-researcher).	6377 words (university researcher) and four interviews with teacher-researcher (Length range 34s – 11m) with 1255 word written reflection.
Student work samples	Collected for all groups.	Collected for all groups.
Pretest-posttest knowledge test	Not applicable.	VR group (n=48), control group (n=134).

(n=48) and non-VR control group (n=134), the latter drawn from the same year level across each campus who undertook the unit of work without the VR component and who were selected for the range equivalency of their pretest knowledge scores (score range 5 to 27).

We also collected handheld video of student interaction and communication in and about iVR including a guided tour by the students of their work in the virtual environment. In addition, we gathered data using: student and teacher interviews and focus groups; student work samples; and screen capture video of student interaction in the virtual environment (Table 4.1). The study was designed to collect data that would illuminate different aspects of learning including declarative knowledge acquisition, effective communication and collaboration, critical thinking and problem-solving, the development of self-directed learning, and other regulatory and metacognitive skills (see chapter 6). Both university researchers and teacher-researchers on each campus collected video and screen capture data during lesson times with the university researcher conducting individual and group interviews with students and teachers.

Dungog High School

A qualitative case study methodology was used at Dungog High School. The study was conducted with a senior Year 11 class (students aged 16–17 years) of nine students (6F, 3M). The research sought to understand how iVR could enhance higher order thinking through a creative design process. Specifically, it explored how the teacher's pedagogical approach leveraged the learning affordances of iVR to develop a deeper understanding of the abstract concept of directorial vision. Data was collected through: handheld video of student interactions; screen capture of students working in the virtual environment; group interviews with students and teachers, and students interviewing others; and student work samples inside and outside of VR. Both the university researcher and teacher-researcher collected handheld video and screen capture data and conducted interviews. Table 4.2 provides an overview of types and scope of the data.

Curriculum Design, Technical Set-up and Procedure

Callaghan College

For phase 2 of the study at Callaghan College, the head teachers of science at each campus worked together to develop a unit of work on the 'Healthy Human Body' from the 'Living World' strand of the New South Wales Science Syllabus of the Australian Curriculum. The learning outcome was: 'A student can analyse interactions between components and processes within biological systems' (New South Wales Education Standards Authority, 2013, p. 16). The syllabus states that through their study of science students, individually and in teams, should: develop

TABLE 4.2 Type and scope of data for Dungog High School research

Type of data	Scope
In-class observational hours	4h 30m
Handheld video recording	1h 59m
Screen capture	1h 50m
Photos of design work in VR	56
Photos of design work outside of VR	53
Student group interviews	19m 50s (100% of participants). Length range 30s – 14m.
Teacher interviews	1hr 12m 32s
Researcher reflection	3506 words (university researcher) and 1876 words (teacher-researcher).
Student work samples	Collected for all groups.

knowledge of scientific concepts and ideas about the living world; gain critical thinking and problem-solving skills; and be able to make evidence-based decisions to communicate understanding and viewpoints. The syllabus allows for the use of digital technologies, including simulations and multi-modal texts, to record, analyse, and present data.

The unit of work developed by the teachers specifically for the study involved a structured online learning module delivered through the learning management system, traditional explicit (didactic) lessons, science labs, and, for the two Year 9 classes assigned to use iVR, a formative assessment task. In this task students chose a body organ to research and represent in VR as a 3D model, cross-section, or diorama. Working in groups of three, students were required to demonstrate their knowledge of the structure and function of the body organ by taking others (students, the teacher, and/or university researcher) on a guided tour of it in iVR. The task aligned well with the learning intent of the syllabus in that it required the group to research, assess, and analyse evidence, and collaborate to develop a model that would educate others. The unit of work for the VR group ran over a 6–7 week period and consisted of 21 x 1 hour lessons with access to iVR for 12 x 1 hour lesson (two of these lessons were partially taken up with pre- and posttesting). The other science students in Year 9, some of whom acted as a control group based on their pretest knowledge scores, undertook the same learning activities in the unit excluding the VR task over 15 x 1 hour lessons (the pedagogical arrangement for the VR and control groups is explained in chapter 6).

The technical set-up at each campus was reasonably similar. Three Oculus Rifts with Touch controllers and VR-ready Alienware laptops were set up in a designated VR room attached to the classroom (see Figures 5.1 and 5.2 in chapter 5). The project could only afford six sets of equipment in all (three for each campus). The 'no code create' sandbox application Minecraft VR (Win 10) was used for the formative assessment task. At one campus Minecraft Win 10 was installed on desktop computers in the classroom (one computer per two students). Students saved their prototypes on USBs to import into the Alienware laptops in the VR room which also had the application. At the other campus students used Minecraft Pocket Edition on their own mobile device that acted as a host server to connect with the Minecraft VR on the Alienware laptops. We chose Minecraft VR as it allowed for a multi-user experience: Students could meet in the virtual environment and work together on their models in a fully interactive way. The engineering properties and tools Minecraft provided were ideal for model creation and some students were already familiar with desktop Minecraft. This hardware and software combination offered all the learning affordances of iVR and these combined with ease of the gestural interface to ensure that students were only limited by their commitment to undertake research and pro- totyping, and their imagination. To minimise the potential for cybersickness and to allow all groups to have fair access to the equipment, students had a maximum of 15 minutes in VR in any one-hour period. This limited access to equipment meant that students needed to plan the use of their time wisely both inside and outside of VR.

Dungog High School

The CAPA head teacher developed a syllabus-aligned unit of work based on the contemporary Australian gothic absurdist play *Ruby Moon* (Cameron, 2005). The play is about the devastating impact of a young girl's disappearance on family and neighbours. Students were to produce a director's folio which would include an immersive vision of the play based on costume and set design elements. Students were to demonstrate an understanding of how the play might be experienced by an audience through this immersive experience (chapter 7 reports on findings).

This project used two Oculus Rifts with Touch controllers and VR-ready Alienware laptops. The 3D drawing program Tilt Brush, a 'no code create' sandbox application, was chosen because it offered all the affordances of an infi- nite virtual design studio. Students could create elements of set and costume designs in 3D, at and beyond scale, and quickly prototype and amend designs according to peer and teacher feedback. They could also navigate around their immersive directorial vision to understand it from different perspectives including how an actor or the audience might experience the design. Tilt Brush is a single- user application and so it was not possible for students to co-create together in the virtual environment. However, the small class size and access to two sets of equipment allowed students to easily cycle in and out of VR. An advantage of Tilt Brush was that it could function offline, an important feature for a rural school where internet bandwidth was an issue. The drama room was a large workshop-style space with portable furniture which could easily accommodate the VR equipment and provide for generous play areas (Figure 5.3 in chapter 5). The unit of work ran over ten weeks with the first five weeks devoted to studying the text, performance, and 'pen and paper' design, and the last five weeks providing access to Tilt Brush so that design elements could be explored and further prototyped in VR. Once the immersive directorial vision was created it was shared with students and teachers. Students had access to 5 x VR lessons that were 52 minutes in length with more time in VR allowed towards the end of the unit if students requested this. The VR equipment was also available at lunchtime with some students taking advantage of this.

Analysis

The methodological approaches, with their rich and varied forms of data collection, allowed for the creation of two in-depth case studies that provided unique insights into the research questions. Case studies have unique analytic and interpretative attributes. They are: particularistic in their focus on a specific context, situation, or phenomenon; useful in their quest for 'thick' detailed description; and heuristic in that they develop or deploy conceptual tools to enhance a deeper understanding of what is being studied (Merriam, 1998). Epistemologically, the research is informed by a social constructivist paradigm that focuses on knowledge production developed through individual and group interaction and influenced by context (Braun and Clarke, 2013). The different types of information collected for each case study allowed for triangulation of data from different sources. This allowed us to draw nuanced and credible conclusions (Miles and Huberman, 1994). Throughout the analytic process emerging findings were subject to a constant dialogic process where the meaning and implications of phenomena were examined by the research team (Russell and Kelly, 2002).

Quantitative Analysis (Callaghan College Only)

Data collected in phase 2 of the Callaghan College study included pretest and posttest scores designed to measure content knowledge acquisition related to the unit of work for all Year 9 students across both campuses. The content knowledge quiz used was the same for both pre- and post-unit testing and included 30 multiple choice questions on facts and concepts related to the 'Healthy Human Body' unit of work. The test was delivered online through the learning management system. Scores for each student were recorded for both the pretest and posttest. Only students who completed both tests were included in the sample with learning gain measured. Learning gain is the difference between the pre- and posttest scores and was recorded as a single number for each student. Statistical tests using SPSS (version 25) were performed to assess the learning gains for each student (Howitt and Cramer, 2017). The first test applied was the statistical significance of the learning gains for the whole group (control and VR groups) reported using the paired t-test. The second test compared the learning gains of the control to the VR group using the independent t-test. Only non-VR students who scored within the same pretest range as the VR group for the knowledge quiz were included in the control group. Results are reported in chapter 6.

Callaghan College phase 2 screen capture video totalled 21:01:49 (hr, min, sec). The screen capture was coded using QSR International's NVivo 12 software. Initial coding categories were: (1) technical difficulties indicated when the video showed that the network, server, program, or tracking system had stopped working; (2) off-task student verbal and non-verbal interaction and behaviour indicated when students, in their assigned groups, were not undertaking activity related to the formative assessment task of building a model of a body organ in VR; (3) on-task student verbal and non-verbal interaction and behaviour where students, in their assigned groups, were undertaking activity directly related to the formative assessment task; (4) on-task student verbal and non-verbal interaction and behaviour where students, working in non-assigned groups, were undertaking activity related to the formative assessment task; (5) video that indicated students interacting with the teacher or researcher who was either in VR or not (Table 4.3).

On-task screen capture video assigned to student groups (10:06:14) was then coded for categories representing types and processes of regulation as outlined in Malmberg, Järvelä, and Järvenoja (2017). The types of regulation were: task execution; goal setting; monitoring and evaluation; planning; strategy use; and task understanding. The regulatory processes were: self-regulation, co-regulation, and socially shared regulation (chapter 6 details provides a description of regulation coding categories and results).

Initially, three researchers undertook three hours of joint coding with a research assistant. Erica Southgate undertook an additional four hours of research coding with the research assistant with the other two researchers also meeting for another four hours to check the accuracy of the coding. At the conclusion of the coding, a random checking of 40% of all on-task video was checked by Erica Southgate to ensure no misinterpretation errors. Only two instances of incorrect interpretation were identified and corrected.

It should be noted that the screen capture did not work consistently across groups and that sometimes the function ceased to work during the lesson for unexplained technical reasons. This resulted in uneven video coverage. All groups of students, however, had some of their in-VR activity videoed. Some groups had more on-task screen capture video than others resulting in data skew. Discussion of results in chapter 6 reflect a cautious approach to interpretation.

TABLE 4.3 Initial categorisation of screen capture video

Screen capture video	Time (hr, min, sec)	% of total video
Technical issues	02:44:19	13.0%
Off-task activity assigned to student group*	05:39:12	27.0%
On-task activity assigned to student group	10:06:14	48.0%
On-task activity not assigned student group	02:26:52	11.6%
Student–researcher/teacher interaction	00:05:12	0.4%

*All off-task activity occurred in student-assigned groups

Qualitative Analysis

This analysis drew on: dialogue from audio and video recordings; field notes; student and teacher interviews; teacher written reflections; and student work samples in and outside of VR. As phase 1 of the Callaghan College study was exploratory, analysis was inductive and followed Miles and Huberman's (1994) three core activities: (1) data was coded and memo-ed according to emerging themes and clusters of phenomena; (2) these were then synthesised and organised into broader categories such as main themes with sub-themes; and then (3) a dialogic approach was used to draw and establish the credibility of conclusions and their implications for the research questions. The Dungog High School data was similarly analysed. Aspects of the Deeper Learning (Noguera, Darling-Hammond, and Friedlaender, 2015) framework were also employed for a more deductive approach to data interpretation. The analytic approach emphasised the role of ongoing reflection and dialogue between university researcher and teacher-researchers, which is a mainstay of participatory research. To ensure the credibility of the interpretation and exemplar selection, all team members discussed emerging findings in meetings and were provided with opportunities to comment on draft papers and chapters in order to assess the extent to which the findings were appropriate and indicative of the phenomena they were intended to exemplify (Punch and Oancea, 2014). Student focus group and interview data triangulated (Jonsen and Jehn, 2009) well with pedagogical themes.

Limitations of the Study

A key method of the Callaghan study was to use screen capture video to record what students did, individually and collectively, in Minecraft VR. The emerging nature of the iVR and its technical failure rate, coupled with the school network and use of variable BYOD student devices, meant that screen capture often stopped working and affected consistency of data collection. Hence, findings should not be treated as representative but rather as a window into the various types of learning behaviour that can occur when students are set a self-directed learning task in a creative and exciting multi-user sandbox environment which is not directly supervised by a teacher. The low socioeconomic status of Callaghan College and Dungog High School communities also means that findings reflect the specific context of financially constrained Western school settings.

Conclusion

This chapter described the purpose, approach, and methodology of the VR School Study conducted at urban Callaghan College junior campuses and rural Dungog High School. These are low-income school communities which made a significant investment in money and teacher time to ensure the success of the research. The study was participatory in its approach, broad in its understanding of what constitutes worthwhile learning, and rich in the collection of different types of data using both quantitative and qualitative methods. It represented the first research of its kind to embed high-end iVR in high school classrooms in a curriculum-aligned manner.

References

Braun, V., & Clarke, V. (2013). *Successful qualitative research.* London: Sage.

Cameron, M. (2005). *Ruby Moon.* Sydney: Currency Press.

Cobbold, T. (2017). What's behind Australia's tottering PISA results: A review of Australia's PISA results. Retrieved http://www.saveourschools.com.au/national-issues/whats-behind-australias-tottering-pisa-results

Howitt, D., & Cramer, D. (2017). *Understanding statistics in psychology with SPSS.* London: Pearson Higher Education.

Jonsen, K., & Jehn, K. A. (2009). Using triangulation to validate themes in qualitative studies. *Qualitative Research in Organizations and Management: An International Journal,* 4(2), 123–150. doi:10.1108/17465640910978391

Kemmis, S., & McTaggart, R. (2008). Participatory action research: Communicative action and the public sphere. In N. K. Denzin & Y. S. Lincoln (Eds.), *Strategies of qualitative inquiry* (pp. 271–330). London: Sage.

Malmberg, J., Järvelä, S., & Järvenoja, H. (2017). Capturing temporal and sequential patterns of self-, co-, and socially shared regulation in the context of collaborative learning. *Contemporary Educational Psychology,* 49, 160–174. doi:10.1016/j.cedpsych.2017.01.009

Merriam, S. B. (1998). *Qualitative research and case study applications in education.* San Francisco: Jossey-Bass.

Miles, M. B., & Huberman, A. M. (1994). *Qualitative data analysis.* Thousand Oaks, CA: Sage.

Noguera, P., Darling-Hammond, L., & Friedlaender, D. (2015). Equal opportunity for Deeper Learning. Jobs for the future. Retrieved https://files.eric.ed.gov/fulltext/ED560802.pdf

New South Wales Education Standards Authority. (2013). *NSW syllabus for the Australian curriculum: Science Year 7–10 syllabus.* Sydney: NSW Education Standards Authority.

Punch, K., & Oancea, A. (2014). *Introduction to research methods in education.* London: Sage.

Russell, G. M., & Kelly, N. H. (2002). Research as interacting dialogic processes: Implications for reflexivity. *Forum Qualitative Social Research,* 3(3), Art.18. doi:10.17169/fqs-3.3.831

Southgate, E., Buchanan, R., Cividino, C., Saxby, S., Eather, G., Bergin, C. ... & Scevak, J. (2018). What teachers should know about highly immersive virtual reality: Insights from the VR School Study. *Scan,* 37(4). Retrieved https://education.nsw.gov.au/teaching-and-learning/professional-learning/scan/past-issues/vol-37/research-highly-immersive-virtual-reality

Southgate, E., Smith, S. P., Cividino, C., Saxby, S., Kilham, J., Eather, G. ... & Bergin, C. (2019). Embedding immersive virtual reality in classrooms: Ethical, organisational and educational lessons in bridging research and practice. *International Journal of Child-Computer Interaction,* 19, 19–29. doi:10.1016/j.ijcci.2018.10.002

5

THE 'NUTS AND BOLTS' OF EMBEDDING IMMERSIVE VIRTUAL REALITY IN CLASSROOMS

Introduction

With the use of iVR in schools still in its infancy, there is value in documenting and reflecting on the 'nuts and bolts' aspects of embedding the technology in the dynamic setting of the classroom. This chapter provides a context-rich account of some of the successes and unintended consequences of the VR School Study. It is an account of the technological 'state of the actual' rather than the 'state of the art' (Selwyn, 2008, p. 83). The chapter begins by describing the practical and technical issues we encountered throughout the study, with a focus on how we responded to ethical conundrums as they arose.

Practical Aspects

Schools are complex organisational environments with most enacting normative ways of organising physical space, dividing time, maintaining knowledge silos known as 'subjects', and planning for and implementing (often inflexible and overcrowded) curriculum. The enduring organisational arrangements of schooling can impede change even when the most enthusiastic of teachers and school leaders are determined to drive innovation (Tyack and Tobin, 1994; Hargreaves and Goodson, 2006).

The term overcrowded curriculum is used to describe the sheer volume of content and skills related to the many mandated subjects that schools must teach. There is often serious pressure on teachers to 'get through the content' and 'check off learning objectives' at the expense of explorative, deeper learning that extends across subject areas. Integration of immersive technology must be curriculum aligned; however, this can be difficult because of an overcrowded curriculum (Southgate and Smith, 2017). Curriculum requirements must be choreographed with the spatio-temporal arrangements that divide and regulate school life (class scheduling, curriculum, and physical space allocated to different disciplines, and related staffing allocations). This can make planning for a new approach to learning very difficult.

At Callaghan College we faced two hurdles during the VR School Study. The first was timetabling the two VR classes in a curriculum-aligned way so that teachers could be confident students had undertaken mandatory coverage of the curriculum. This included ensuring that the study phase 2 control group, drawn from the entire Year 9 student cohort on both campuses, undertook the same unit of work at the same time as the VR groups. The second was finding classrooms that had enough space to accommodate the three Oculus Rifts with their tracking systems and play areas ample enough to accommodate relatively free arm movement and more restricted leg movement. Schools are generally built according to industrial era specifications: They accommodate rows or groups of desks with little room for any other equipment. At Callaghan College there were no available classrooms large enough to accommodate the VR equipment in the actual classroom space and so a solution was to use classrooms with an extra space attached to it. On one campus this extra space was a snug storeroom (4m x 3m) (Figure 5.1) attached to a classroom which the teachers made safe by partitioning

FIGURE 5.1 The storeroom which became the VR room on one campus of Callaghan College

the play areas with padded cubical divider and fixing soft mats to the walls. At the other campus it was a more generous former lab preparation area (5m x 5m) (Figure 5.2) attached to the classroom. These spaces became proudly known in the schools as the VR rooms.

At Dungog High School we did not encounter the same spatio-temporal issues as Callaghan College. A small senior class (n=9) participated in the study and there was adequate existing timetable allowance for the project. In addition, drama classes were conducted in a large workshop-style classroom that easily accommodated the two sets of VR equipment with generous play areas (Figure 5.3). This was the ideal because we wanted to use the 3D drawing program Tilt Brush as a virtual studio that could allow students to design at-scale set elements and costumes in a naturally embodied manner by fully utilising the gestural interface to paint in 3D.

Allowing students enough time to acclimatise to highly iVR presented challenges at Callaghan College because we had limited designated VR lessons per week and only three units of VR equipment per class per campus. That meant there were three sets of iVR equipment per 27–30 students. As we were introducing a new technology several lessons were required to: induct each group of students into using the equipment safely; allow time for students to get used to using the equipment including the controllers; and familiarise themselves with the intensity and wonder of

FIGURE 5.2 The former lab preparation area that became a VR room at the other campus of Callaghan College

FIGURE 5.3 Partial view of the Dungog drama room with teacher Louise Rowley and students

the highly immersive virtual environment, Minecraft VR, that they were to use in the learning task. The importance of play in this process cannot be overstated (Southgate et al., 2018). This was especially true for girls at Callaghan College who, prior to the study, were more likely to have had *no* experience of iVR compared with boys and were much less likely to have played with technology on multiple occasions compared to their male peers (Table 5.1). Only one student (a girl) at Dungog High School had tried iVR (her cousin's PlayStation VR) prior to the study.

In phase 1 of the study, a small number of girls (n=4) at Callaghan College expressed reluctance to try VR. These girls conveyed embarrassment at wearing the headset and would only try it on if they were positioned in the VR room out of sight from their peers in the main classroom. In phase 2 of the study, four girls decided they did not like the 'feeling' of being in VR and instead undertook work on the learning task via desktop computer or mobile device. In mixed groups, girls who did not like iVR undertook much of the research and design work outside of iVR, while boys in the group did the building in iVR. This

TABLE 5.1 Number of times students had tried iVR prior to study by sex of participant

Times in VR with HMD by phase (P)	P1 male	P2 male	Male total	P1 female	P2 female	Female total
0	5	12	17	14	12	26
1–2	19	6	25	6	6	12
3–4	5	3	8	1	1	2
More than 4	3	6	9	1	2	3

division of labour impacted on the learning of boys who were not able to articulate, with the same level of expertise, the structure and function of the model of the body organ that the group developed. Although only a small number of girls expressed reluctance to try iVR and to work in it on the learning task, this phenomenon was not apparent amongst boys.

There is substantial evidence of the persistent underrepresentation of girls and women in STEM subjects and professions (Broadley, 2015; Archer and DeWitt, 2015). In Australia, 84% of people with a STEM qualification are male (Office of the Chief Scientist, 2018). By age 14, girls are less likely than boys to aspire to science careers (Archer, 2013). The self-conscious reaction of some girls to VR could be considered normative gendered behaviour (Tolman, Davis, and Bowman, 2016). There is significant research on how girls and women are socialised into managing their bodily presence to avoid the male gaze and maintain normative notions of an emphasised femininity (Young, 2005). Wearing a large (unattractive) headset that blocks out the user's ability to see (and even hear) what is going on in the outside world can make some girls feel uncomfortable.

Most girls in our study had very little prior exposure to iVR compared to boys. Providing early, sustained opportunities for girls to play with emerging technology will both demystify it and hopefully make it less 'embarrassing'. It is worth reflecting that although we could not integrate the VR equipment into the existing classroom space, situating it in an adjoining room may have been of benefit to some girls as it provided them a relatively private experience in first trying out the technology.

Technical Aspects

While carving out time and space to conduct the study within the organisational context of schools proved challenging, perhaps the most difficult aspect of the study was getting the technology to work reliably during lesson time and within the constraints of the government-run network. This was particularly apparent at Callaghan College where we needed to use a networked application. The Department of Education's network blocked access to the Oculus game store (and other game stores) that would have easily enabled the multiple-player mode option for Minecraft VR (Win 10). We needed to bring in a modem to establish a networked Wi-Fi hot spot outside of the Department's network to enable a multi-user virtual environment. The connectivity would drop out in unpredictable ways during lessons and we were not able to fix this. There were also issues with Minecraft freezing, the VR tracking system functioning incorrectly and the need to keep reconfiguring the Guardian system, all of which interrupted learning time in iVR and could be demotivating for some students (Table 4.3 in chapter 4 indicates lost learning time due to technical issues). It took a significant amount of teacher time to set up external individual user accounts for students required to run a networked version of Minecraft VR with the Oculus Rift.

These ongoing issues meant that teachers spent considerable time trying to resolve technical issues rather than assisting students with the learning task.

Each campus of Callaghan College had access to different hardware. At one school the set up involved students sharing desktop computers located in the classroom to research and create their models before putting these on a USB and loading them into Minecraft VR. At the other school, the classroom did not have any desktop computers and the set of iPads at the school was booked out, so students needed to use their own mobile device (usually a smartphone) for the study. Students used the Pocket Edition of Minecraft which was compatible with the Minecraft VR (Win 10 version). The student's mobile devices acted as a server to host the Minecraft world in which their model was created with other students going into the world via Minecraft VR through the Oculus Rifts. Students from low socioeconomic status backgrounds do not have the latest or best technology or sufficient data for their educational needs (Livingstone and Helsper, 2007). The variability in quality of student Bring-your-own-device (BYOD) devices at this campus acted as a barrier to smooth implementation. One teacher summed this up in an interview conducted at the end of the study:

> It's been fun. Arduous probably comes to mind as well ... The biggest issues weren't so much around the pedagogy. All the teachers that were involved had really good ideas on how to implement to VR into it [the curriculum]. It was more the technology side [such as] learning to work within the Department's ... network and then there's the hurdle of kids' access to technology because a lot of kids don't have the technology [mobile computing devices] to bring and the ones that perhaps do, it might not be the right type of equipment for the project. And then when we do have devices to offer the students it's then trying to install the software because there are policy restrictions [from the Department] ... on the devices so we need to find ways around that. And interesting things like copying a [Minecraft] world from a [mobile] device to a laptop when connectivity is not all it should be, stopping and restarting servers, and keeping kids on track when their devices aren't working.

If the student with the BYOD mobile device hosting the Minecraft world was away for the VR lesson other students in their group would not have access to the model. Similarly, the shared accounts with students using Minecraft VR on the desktop computers created problems if a student was absent, with their peers needing to text them for login details so that they could continue work on their model. The use of smartphones as a practical solution to enable wireless networking may have contributed to some of the technical issues that arose at one school, particularly Minecraft freezing and the network dropping out, although this was also apparent at the other school. Although the screen capture video was an imperfect representation of student time in iVR, it did indicate that there were technical issues at least 13% of the time.

Dungog High School used Tilt Brush in offline mode because they were also unable to access the program online because of departmental network restrictions. As a rural school they also had to consider use of bandwidth. Teachers had to take computing equipment home to update programs.

It is understandable that school systems enforce restrictions on internet access. However, this highlighted the difficulties of using commercial-of-the-shelf software that requires access to the internet for multi-user mode, updates, and downloadable content and licence validation. Moreover, in these low income school communities there were simply not enough desktop or sets of mobile computing equipment for 1–1 access, and BYOD policies meant that many students had a less than optimal smart phone to undertake work on. The problems we encountered indicated that school systems may not be technically agile enough or adequately resourced to support innovative learning projects.

Ethical Aspects

Some of the most valuable lessons from the study were ethical in nature and would not have come about if we had not incubated iVR in actual classrooms. There was (and still is) limited research and evidence-informed resources on the ethical use of immersive technologies with children and young people (chapter 2 reviews ethical and legal considerations of iVR). Without a model or existing resources to draw on, we spent a year investigating the ethical dimensions of using the technology in schools and developing safety and ethics protocols and resources for the study. Research ethics should be conceived as procedural (that is part of an institutional approval process) and as ethics-in-practice (Guillemin and Gillam, 2004). Ethics in-practice involves enacting real-time sensitivity and awareness through observation to inform judgements and decision-making in the field (Phelan and Kinsella, 2013).

During the procedural ethics phase we developed protocols and resources to mitigate against potential harm prior to conducting data collection. Our participant invitation pack contained a plain English information statement and parent/carer consent and child assent form, and a screening questionnaire designed to educate parents and students about the potential risks of iVR (cybersickness and potential health conditions that might be incompatible with an immersive experience). To minimise the likelihood of cybersickness we limited VR time to 15–20 minutes per student within a one to two hour period and no student used VR during the last lesson of the day in case of an adverse reaction. Although there are engineered approaches to creating virtual environments that minimise the potential for cybersickness (Porcino, Clua, Trevisan, Vasconcelos, and Valente, 2017), it is not possible to predict if an individual will experience this in VR. Hence, we took an educative approach by producing a teacher safety talk script to be delivered at the beginning of the project and a 'Be VR Aware' safety poster to display in the VR rooms (Figure 5.4). The teacher and the researcher also regularly checked in with students to make sure they felt fine while in VR.

FIGURE 5.4 'Be VR Aware' classroom poster

Ethics-in-practice is especially important when introducing a new technology as some issues could not have been anticipated during the procedural ethics stage. For example, it became apparent that there was a need for someone in the VR rooms to act as a 'spotter' to ensure that students did not collide with objects or people. The Guardian system, a virtual grid warning system built into the Oculus environment to highlight safe boundaries for play, was not always effective in ensuring students kept within the safe area. Some students became so immersed that they either ignored the Guardian system or moved too quickly to respond to it; hence, the need for a person to assume a watchful eye. The 'spotter' was either the university-researcher or another student. The teacher did not undertake the role because they were needed in the adjoining classroom with the majority of students. This arrangement highlighted the bind of not having a classroom space large enough to accommodate iVR with adequately sized play areas where supervision might be easier.

Perhaps the most important ethics-in-practice insight was produced as a result of a conversation between Chris Cividino of Callaghan College and myself when we identified the child protection implication of using VR equipment in schools. Australian school systems operate according to child protection laws, policies, and procedures that entail protecting children from violence and maintaining a safe and respectful environment. When using a VR headset, a person is either in darkness while they are waiting for an application to load or in the virtual world. They cannot see what is going on outside of the headset or who is near them. While there are some high-end headsets with cameras that allow the user to 'see through' into the real world, these were rare during our study. The need to help students fit the VR equipment (either initially or in an ongoing manner) and the inability of users to see what is going on outside the headset raisesd child protection issues. It was often the 'spotters' role during the study to help guide students in VR back into a safe position in the play area, especially in the more confined VR room. Respectful interaction with students while they have the headset on is vital. This includes those who might be touch-sensitive such as students from diverse cultural backgrounds, those with special needs, or with life experiences that make them avoid physical contact. With the teacher, university-researcher, and other students all assisting with the fitting of equipment and ensuring students in VR did not make contact with objects or other people, we determined a need to develop a simple protocol in classroom poster form that would assist with respectful interaction (Figure 5.5).

Conclusion

This chapter has provided a fine-grained account of the 'nuts and bolts' aspects of embedding iVR in to the natural setting of the school classroom, a topic that has received inadequate attention (Hew and Cheung, 2010). Our experience suggests that one of the most vital elements when introducing and researching an emerging technology into schools is time. The most difficult aspect of the study at Callaghan College was in the negotiation of existing timetabling, spatial, and technological (network and computing device) arrangements. As Pellas et al. (2017) observe, computer hardware and server requirements can create substantial

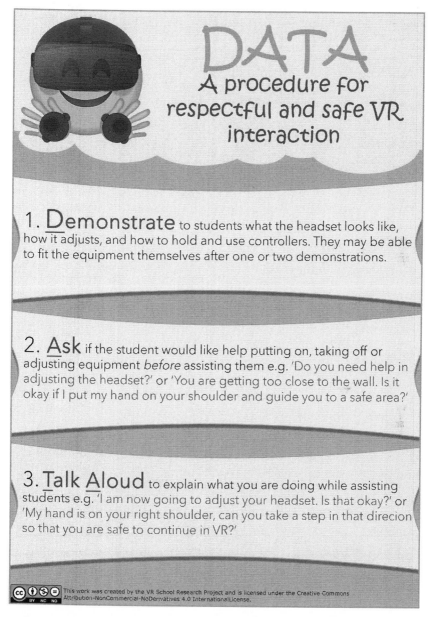

FIGURE 5.5 DATA procedure poster for respectful and safe VR interaction

technological-operational drawbacks to implementing VR in the classroom. This was reinforced by one teacher who remarked: 'The pedagogical aspects of the research were the least of our problems.' During the study, we took time to communicate with and educate students and their parents/carers about iVR, its unique learning affordances, and its potential harms, and created new protocols and resources to address ethical and safety issues as they emerged. This involved an ethical commitment by the university-researcher to spend considerable time 'in the field', not as a detached scientist enacting an experiment but as a responsible researcher-educator collaborating with teachers to ensure student welfare and quality learning opportunities for all.

References

Archer, L. (2013). *ASPIRES: Young people's science and career aspirations, aged 10–14. Report.* London: King's College London.

Archer, L., & DeWitt, J. (2015). Science aspirations and gender identity: Lessons from the ASPIRES project. In E. K. Henriksen, J. Dillon, & J. Ryder (Eds.), *Understanding student participation and choice in science and technology education* (pp. 89–102). Dordrecht, the Netherlands: Springer.

Broadley, K. (2015). Entrenched gendered pathways in science, technology, engineering and mathematics: Engaging girls through collaborative career development. *Australian Journal of Career Development,* 24(1), 27–38. doi:10.1177%2F1038416214559548

Guillemin, M., & Gillam, L. (2004). Ethics, reflexivity, and 'ethically important moments' in research. *Qualitative Inquiry,* 10(2), 261–280. doi:10.1177%2F1077800403262360

Hargreaves, A., & Goodson, I. (2006). Educational change over time? The sustainability and nonsustainability of three decades of secondary school change and continuity. *Education Administration Quarterly,* 42(1), 3–41. doi:10.1177%2F0013161X05277975

Hew, K. F., & Cheung, W. S. (2010). Use of three-dimensional (3-D) immersive virtual worlds in K-12 and higher education settings: A review of the research. *British Journal of Educational Technology,* 41(1), 33–55. doi:10.1111/j.1467-8535.2008.00900.x

Livingstone, S., & Helsper, E. (2007). Gradations in digital inclusion: Children, young people and the digital divide. *New Media & Society,* 9(4) 671–696. doi:10.1177% 2F1461444807080335

Office of the Chief Scientist. (2018). *Australia's STEM workforce: Science, technology, engineering and mathematics report.* Canberra: Australian Government. Retrieved https://www.chiefscientist.gov.au/wp-content/uploads/Australias-STEM-workforce_full-report.pdf

Pellas, N., Kazanidis, I., Konstantinou, N., & Georgiou, G. (2017). Exploring the educational potential of three-dimensional multi-user virtual worlds for STEM education: A mixed-method systematic literature review. *Education and Information Technologies,* 22(5), 2235–2279. doi:10.1007/s10639-016-9537-2

Phelan, S.K., & Kinsella, E. A. (2013). Picture this ... Safety, dignity, and voice – ethical research with children: Practical considerations for the reflexive researcher. *Qualitative Inquiry,* 19(2), 81–90. doi:10.1177%2F1077800412462987

Porcino, T. M., Clua, E., Trevisan, D., Vasconcelos, C. N., & Valente, L. (2017). Minimizing cyber sickness in head mounted display systems: design guidelines and applications. In *2017 IEEE 5th International Conference on Serious Games and Applications for Health (SeGAH)* (pp. 1–6). New York: IEEE. doi:10.1109/SeGAH.2017.7939283

Selwyn, N. (2008) From state-of-the-art to state-of-the-actual? Introduction to a special issue. *Technology, Pedagogy and Education,* 17(2), 83–87. doi:10.1080/14759390802098573

Southgate, E., & Smith, S. P. (2017). Designing and conducting research using immersive technologies in schools: Seven observations. In *2017 IEEE Virtual Reality Workshop on*

K-12 Embodied Learning through Virtual & Augmented Reality (KELVAR) (pp. 1–3). New York: IEEE. doi:10.1109/KELVAR.2017.7961564

Southgate, E., Buchanan, R., Cividino, C., Saxby, S., Eather, G., Bergin, C. … & Scevak, J. (2018). What teachers should know about highly immersive virtual reality: Insights from the VR School Study. *Scan*, 37(4). Retrieved https://education.nsw.gov.au/tea ching-and-learning/professional-learning/scan/past-issues/vol-37/research-highly-imme rsive-virtual-reality

Tolman, D. L., Davis, B. R., & Bowman, C. P. (2016). "That's just how it is" A gendered analysis of masculinity and femininity ideologies in adolescent girls' and boys' heterosexual relationships. *Journal of Adolescent Research*, 31(1), 3–31. doi:10.1177%2F0743558415587325

Tyack, D., & Tobin, W. (1994). The 'grammar' of schooling: Why has it been so hard to change? *American Educational Research Journal*, 31(3), 453–479. doi:10.3102%2F00028312031003453

Young, I. M. (2005). *On female body experience: 'Throwing like a girl' and other essays*. Oxford: Oxford University Press.

6

'IT MAKES YOU ACTUALLY INTERACT WITH THE THINGS YOU ARE LEARNING ABOUT'

Secondary School Science Through Immersive Virtual Reality

This chapter has been written with contributions by Callaghan College teachers Shane Saxby, Jivv Kilham, Chris Cividino, Graham Eather, Amy Worth, Candece Bergin, and David Summerville, and University of Newcastle researchers Susan Grimes, Jill Scevak, and Kathleen Smithers.

Introduction

This chapter reports on findings from a multi-site, mixed method study that used Minecraft VR for learning about biology in junior secondary school. The study represents the first research of its kind to investigate embedding the technology in the natural setting of the classroom as an extension of curriculum and teacher practice. This chapter draws on quantitative and qualitative data to build a nuanced picture of the pedagogical approach to employing iVR in science classes and what student learning, in all its complexity, looked like in the study.

The chapter begins by outlining the context and scope of the study from a learning perspective. It then goes on to describe the curriculum approach to using iVR in science class and the technical set up. This is followed by an overview of three different perspectives on learning that were explored in the study to provide new insights into how students used the iVR sandbox of Minecraft VR to undertake a formative assessment task. The focus then shifts to describing research findings related to: content knowledge acquisition; regulation of learning in Minecraft VR; and aspects of Deeper Learning (Noguera, Darling-Hammond, and Friedlaender, 2015) from the viewpoint of students and teachers.

Study Context, Curriculum Approach, and Technical Aspects

Callaghan College is a low-income high school community located in Newcastle, New South Wales, Australia. It consists of two junior and one senior campus. This chapter reports on the 2018 phase of the VR School Study which used Minecraft VR in two mixed-ability Year 9 science classes at the junior college campuses (see chapter 4 for the methodology and sample). Callaghan College emphasises technology-enhanced learning and the study was supported by the college principal and members of the Future Learning Team who are co-authors of this chapter.

The science head teachers from each campus developed a unit of work on the 'Healthy Human Body' from the 'Living World' strand of the New South Wales Science Syllabus for the Australian Curriculum. The learning outcome was: 'A student can analyse interactions between components and processes within biological systems' (NSW Education Standards Authority, 2013, p. 16). The syllabus also mandated that: students develop knowledge of scientific concepts and ideas about the living world; work scientifically to plan and conduct investigations to develop their understanding of scientific concepts and skills in critical thinking and problem-solving; gain experience in making evidence-based decisions; and be able to communicate their understanding and viewpoints.

The unit of work involved the entire Year 9 cohort on both campuses. All students undertook online learning via a teacher-developed module and in traditional explicit (didactic) lessons and science labs; and for the two Year 9 classes assigned to use iVR, a formative assessment task using Minecraft VR. Formative assessment is lower-stakes evaluation of student progress and mastery of learning objectives and is not typically graded. Table 6.1 provides an overview of the pedagogical structure of the unit of work for the VR group and non-VR (control) group.

The formative assessment task involved students, in groups of three, undertaking their own online research to build a 3D model, cross-section, or diorama of a body organ of their choice using the 'no code create' sandbox of Minecraft VR. Minecraft VR is a multi-user environment which means that students could work together within the virtual world for 15–20 minutes at a time before handing the equipment over to the next group. Each group was required to demonstrate research and knowledge about structure and function of their chosen body organ by taking others (peers, teacher, and/or university researcher) on a guided tour of it in VR.

The study could only afford six sets of equipment (three for each campus). Three Oculus Rifts with Touch controllers and VR-ready Alienware laptops were set up in rooms attached to the main classrooms (Figures 5.1 and 5.2 in chapter 5). The unit of work ran over a 6–7 week period. The VR classes had 21 x 1 hour lessons with access to the VR equipment for 12 x 1 hour lesson (57% of all lessons). As access to time in VR was limited, students developed prototypes of their model in screen-based Minecraft. They needed to manage their project carefully to maximise outcomes in VR.

TABLE 6.1 Pedagogical and assessment structure of the Year 9 biology unit of work

Control (Non-VR group)	VR group
- Summative assessment knowledge test. - Formative assessment related to lab work.	- Summative assessment knowledge test. - Formative assessment related to lab work. - Formative assessment VR task: Collaboratively select and research a body organ, prototype a model of it in desktop Minecraft and develop it further in iVR to take others on an educational tour of it.
15 x 1 hr lessons of explicit (didactic) pedagogy, online learning module developed for project, and labs.	9 x 1 hr lessons of explicit (didactic) pedagogy and labs.
	12 x 1 hr lessons with access to: desktop computers or BYOD devices to research the body organ and screen-build the organ in Minecraft Win 10 or Pocket Edition; Oculus Rifts with Touch controllers with VR-ready Alienware laptops (3 sets of VR equipment per campus); and online learning module developed for the unit of work.

There were two main reasons why the VR task was formative rather than summative assessment. Firstly, as Table 5.1 (in chapter 5) illustrates, most students had never tried iVR, especially the girls. The experimental nature of using an emerging technology in school classrooms and the steep technical and task learning curve meant that it would have been unfair to make it a high-stakes, graded task. Secondly, the findings from the previous phase of the study (reported in chapter 5), and later supported by this phase of the research, indicated that the technology was unlikely to work reliably every lesson which was stressful enough for the teachers and university researcher without transferring this to students.

Understanding Learning Through iVR From Different Perspectives

Most studies on using iVR for learning restrict themselves to measuring lower order content knowledge acquisition (Jensen and Konradsen, 2018): In other words, whether students remembered factual information (content knowledge) as a result of experiencing a virtual environment or doing a learning task in VR. This is often ascertained with a pre- and post-knowledge test, sometimes with a control (equivalent comparison) group who learn the same content matter but without the iVR experience. It is valuable to determine if the use of a technology assists with learning content (often described in term of learning gain), especially if this is compared with a traditional pedagogical approach. The Callaghan College study did measure content knowledge gain and there was an equivalent (control) group for comparative purposes. However, we were also interested in understanding learning as a complex, social phenomenon using a broad gamut of perspectives that included, but extended beyond, lower order content knowledge acquisition.

We used three additional foci to understand learning through iVR: (1) time spent on-task; (2) regulatory behaviour and its related concept of metacognition; and (3) the student experience of aspects associated with the Deeper Learning framework (Noguera, Darling-Hammond, and Friedlaender, 2015). The research also aimed to understand the broader implications for embedding an emerging immersive technology into the classroom from an pedagogical perspective. Thus, in addition to pre- and posttest content knowledge scores, the study collected: handheld video and sound recordings of student interaction and communication in the VR room; student and teacher interview and focus groups data; student work samples from Minecraft VR; and screen capture video of student interaction in the virtual environment (see Table 4.1 in chapter 4).

Ideally, the non-VR (control) group should have undertaken the same model building task but using 2D Minecraft via a computer/device screen. If this occurred the research could have examined the impact of iVR versus 2D model building on learning outcomes. However, this was not feasible due to a lack of access to desktop computers or class sets of mobile devices at the schools and an absence of or huge variability in the quality of student BYOD devices, a reflection of the schools' low-income status.

Content Knowledge Acquisition

The head teachers of science, who also taught the VR class on their respective campus, developed a pre- and post-knowledge test comprising 30 identical multiple choice questions on facts and concepts from the biology unit of work. The pre- and posttest knowledge quiz did not include any questions on the formative VR assessment task which was based on students' own research on a body organ of their choice. The pre- and post-knowledge tests were administered as online quizzes through the learning management system to all Year 9 students on both campuses. For this component of the study there was the VR group of mixed-ability Year 9 students (n=48) and non-VR control group of mixed-ability Year 9 students (n=134). In all, there were matched completed pre- and post-knowledge tests for 182 Year 9 students across both campuses.

The biology content for the unit of work was identical for both the VR group and non-VR (control) group. However, the unit of work for the VR group comprised 21 lessons of which 12 were set aside for researching their body organ of choice and building it in VR, while the non-VR (control) group undertook the unit of work across 15 lessons. Therefore, the non-VR group had more exposure to traditional didactic lessons on the content of the test than the VR group while the VR group had more lessons set aside for flexible self-directed online learning and research and development of their VR model.

In order to assess statistical significance, the data was cleaned with only valid pretest and posttest pairs included. The pretest score range for the VR class (5 to 27) was used to select the control group from the Year 9 non-VR control data supplied by the schools. The whole sample (n=182) showed content knowledge learning gain (Table 6.2). Statistical analysis using the t-test to compare the pretest and posttest scores showed that there were statistically significant differences between pre- and post-unit learning for the whole sample (p=0.0000).

Comparison between the VR and control classes using the independent t-test showed no statistical significance between the learning gains (p=0.700) (Table 6.3).

While the majority of students recorded learning gain, some students in both VR and non-VR groups recorded negative gains in the posttest. This may have been due to disengagement in science or, more likely, inattention and distraction on the day of the posttest which was undertaken in classes in which it was not always possible to set aside quiet time to undertake the quiz. The content knowledge result is not surprising.

Although students in the VR class did not learn any more content knowledge (facts and concepts) than their non-VR peers, they certainly did not learn any less. This was despite being given less traditional explicit (didactic) instructional lesson time and an extra, complex learning task to undertake which required self-regulated, higher order thinking, and collaboration using a new technology. Although the VR group had six extra lessons compared with the control group, students in the VR classes no doubt encountered a high cognitive load (Sweller, 1988). This involved both intrinsic cognitive load (or getting to grips with the demands of a complex task that required extensive intellectual engagement through research and modes of symbolic representation) and extrinsic cognitive load (or the demands of learning how master the technology and harness the learning affordances of Minecraft VR to improve the educational benefit of their model in the guided experience of it). To elaborate, in addition to undertaking learning via the online module and in

TABLE 6.2 Knowledge test score paired t-test for whole sample

N=182	Mean	SD
Pretest	15.40	4.957
Posttest	19.86	5.856

TABLE 6.3 Knowledge test comparison between VR group and control group

Group	n=	Pretest	Posttest	Learning gain	Gain range	SD gain
VR	48	16.38	21.08	4.71	–3 to 18	4.443
Control	134	15.04	19.42	4.37	–11 to 18	5.364
All	182	15.40	19.86	4.44	–11 to 18	5.131

TABLE 6.4 Time on- and off-task by group

Group	Total time	Off-task time	On-task time	% of time on-task
Eye 1	00:48:12	00:32:06	00:16:06	33.40%
Eye 2	01:05:19	00:01:34	01:03:45	97.60%
Eye 3	00:27:41	00:16:44	00:10:57	39.55%
Eye 4	01:07:06	00:28:22	00:38:44	57.72%
Eye 5	01:48:12	00:29.00	01:19:12	73.19%
Eye 6	00:47:54	00:08:48	00:39:06	81.62%
Artery	01:04:06	00:04:18	00:59:48	93.29%
Vein/Artery	01:38:04	01:23.02	00:15:02	15.32%
Brain 1	01:53:54	00:14:48	01:39:06	87.00%
Brain 2	00:43:48	00:20:12	00:23:36	53.88%
Skin 1	00:59:18	00:10:09	00:49.09	82.88%
Skin 2	01:11:03	00:47:02	00:24:01	33.80%
Stomach	00:13:15	00:01:07	00:12:08	91.57%
Tongue	00:41:11	00:00:09	00:41:02	99.63%
Heart	00:52:04	00:17:32	00:34:32	66.30%
Lava*	00:24:19	00:24:19	00:00:00	0.0%

*This group of three boys had a propensity for building structures and burning them down with lava.

traditional science classes and labs, the VR students, within a short window of six hours, also needed to ensure that they: (1) collaboratively functioned as a group; (2) undertook extra content knowledge acquisition through self-directed online research so that their model and guided to tour of it was factually correct; (3) technically mastered an unfamiliar technology to develop an understanding of its pedagogical potential in 3D model building; and (4) enacted cycles of prototyping inside and outside of VR. They were also required to use their imaginations to push the boundaries of learning science through symbolic and creative endeavour.

While the pre- and post-knowledge test did not assess content knowledge related to researching and creating the body organ model or self-directed learning, teamwork, or the range of communication skills required for the task, we included other methods to collect data on these learning outcomes. The next section describes how students went about learning in Minecraft VR, with an emphasis on time-on-task, regulatory behaviours, and how the student experience reflected aspects of Deeper Learning (Noguera, Darling-Hammond, and Friedlaender, 2015).

On- and Off-Task Behaviour in iVR

Experiencing an immersive virtual world like Minecraft VR, with its unique, evocative moods and amazing modes of navigation and interaction, can be overwhelming and distracting especially if a student is new to iVR and multi-user environments. These types of immersive worlds are veritable playgrounds designed to spark the imagination and excite the senses with a full range of interactive possibilities. When we asked students to go into a virtual world to undertake a learning task there was a possibility that they might experience cognitive overload (Sweller, 2005) and spend more time interacting for leisure than for learning. The phenomenon of time-on-task behaviour has been explored in educational research mostly using observation schedules which seek to describe the frequency, forms, and correlates of such behaviour (Beserra, Nussbaum, and Oteo, 2019; Godwin, Almeda, Seltman, Kai, Skerbetz, Baker, and Fisher, 2016). While there is a literature that describes learning in screen-based virtual worlds (Hunsinger and Krotoski, 2013), we were unable to locate studies on time-on-task behaviour in screen-based VR or as it might naturally occur in iVR environments. To address this, screen capture video of students in Minecraft VR was recorded and coded for on- and off-task behaviour and a range of regulatory (metacognitive) behaviours.

Screen capture is a video recording of what is happening on the computer screen; in this case, the way students in first-person view navigate and interact in the virtual environment of Minecraft VR. It involved pressing the Windows + G keys on each of the laptop computers (popularly known as the game bar because it is used by computer gamers to record gameplay). This function recorded what students were doing, by themselves and with others, in iVR. An icon showing that the screen was recording would appear on the screen. If three students in the group were all in Minecraft together, this captured both individual and group action from the visual and audio perspective. The university researcher, teachers, and students were all cognisant that the screen capture should be activated prior to each group going into Minecraft (although this was not always successful in practice).

On-task behaviour was defined as when students, individually and in groups, undertook actions in the virtual environment that directly related to the learning task of prototyping, building, adjusting, and evaluating the body organ model in Minecraft VR. Off-task behaviour included actions that were not related to the learning task such as exploring and getting lost in the virtual world (on foot or by swimming or flying), herding, riding, or killing virtual animals, building and destroying objects that had no relationship to the learning task, setting off fireworks, and play-fighting.

In all, 21:01:49 (hours, minutes, seconds) of screen capture video was recorded (Table 4.3 in chapter 4). Theoretically, it should have been possible to screen capture 72 hours of student activity in VR (12 hours of VR-accessible lesson time x 6 sets of VR equipment/laptops). However, at a minimum approximately 20% (14:24:00) of potential student activity in VR time would have been taken up with arrival to class, change-over of groups and pack-up time, and time lost to technical issues. Realistically, the best estimate for possible screen capture of all student activity in VR would have been 57:36:00. We did not manage to collect this amount of video. Occasionally, the screen capture ceased functioning due to unexplained technical reasons and participants did not notice this to restart it. At other times the dynamic nature of the classroom environment meant that we forgot to switch it on.

During the initial round of analysis, screen capture video was coded in QSR International's NVivo 12 software. Initial categories were: technical issues (network drop out, unexplained program stoppage, or VR tracking or Guardian failure); interactions between students and the researcher/teacher; and on- or off-task behaviour (Table 4.3 in chapter 4; see chapter 4 for a description of the analysis).

Deducting screen capture time for technical issues and researcher/teacher interaction, the study collected 18:12:18 of video showing student activity in VR (Table 4.3 in chapter 4). Based on the realistic estimate of a potential for a total of 57:36:00 of video of student activity in VR, our data set comprised approximately 31.60% of possible screen capture video of student interaction (excluding the time for student-teacher/researcher interaction).

Of the 18:12:18 screen capture of student activity in VR, 68.95% (12:33:06) of the video showed on-task learning and 31.05% (05:39:12) depicted off-task behaviour. It should be noted that sometimes students joined classmates in VR who were not part of their assigned group because a group member was away for the lesson and they decided to join in as there was a spare headset available. Only on-task screen capture video that could be attributed to students working in their assigned groups in VR (10:06:14) was coded for processes and types of learning regulation (findings presented in the next section of this chapter). This represented 25.35% of total possible screen capture of student activity in VR.

We collected screen capture video for all groups. However, the imperfect nature of the screen capture video coverage, including for each group (range from 00:13:15 to 01:53:54) (Table 6.4), meant that it should not be treated as representative. That said, it was possible to triangulate (Denzin, 2012) insights from the screen capture analysis with researcher observations, the quality of student work samples (models in Minecraft), and student and teacher interviews, to increase the credibility of findings and enhance insight into what can happen when students set about learning in highly immersive virtual environments.

For example, it was not surprising that the group known as Eye 2 were almost 100% on-task: They also had very high levels of social-shared regulation or highly collaborative behaviour (Table 6.8). This group produced an elaborate educational experience which involved a model of an enormous eye that was toured by boarding a cart on an automated roller coaster that went along the ground beside the eye and stopped at fun facts about the eye which were on placards in the ground (one placard read, 'The white bit in the eyeball is called the sclera'). After reading the placards the learner-tourist could reactivate the cart to glide up into the eye's cavernous interior which was correctly anatomically labelled (for example a sign on the optic nerve said, 'This transmits pulses from the brain to the retina'). The learner-tourist then pulled a lever to hurtle through the optic nerve to go outside of the eye where the cart made its way back along the rails to a custom-built station where the learner-tourist dismounted the cart to proceed down a staircase and up a ladder until they reached a high viewing platform to take in the model in its entirety (Figure 6.1 provides an external glimpse of the

FIGURE 6.1 Screenshot of roller coaster eye model with factual placards (foreground) and optic nerve at rear that served as the exit point after riding through the eye's interior

elaborate structure). It was an exuberant, informative, and slightly nauseating educational experience.

After triangulation, the only obvious anomalies were that of the Heart, Vein/ Artery, and Lava groups. To clarify, the 66% on-task figure for the Heart Group, consisting of three girls who created an elaborate internal model of the human heart based on comprehensive research, is almost certainly an underestimation. The heart had to be toured internally in the same direction blood moves through its four chambers with this symbolised with flowing 'blood'. Detailed and accurate 'fun fact' annotations could be found on the internal walls of the heart's chambers. The tour was claustrophobic, incredibly detailed, and fascinating at the same time.

Likewise the screen capture for the Vein/Artery group, consisting of three girls, both underestimates on-task activity and suggests that this group completed the task at a highly competent level more quickly than their peers. The Vein/Artery Group developed a very interesting annotated model where the learner-tourist travelled in the correct direction of blood flow through the vein or artery: The girls suggested that the learner-tourist should think of themselves as a 'platelet' when undertaking the tour. The screen capture video for this group mainly related to the end of the unit of work and showed that the girls spent a significant amount of time playing in and around their model by shooting off fireworks and experimenting with the properties of lava (but not in a destructive way). The Lava group, consisting of three boys, exhibited exemplary collaborative skills when exploring and building complex houses and towers in Minecraft VR only to work together to destroy them in spectacular manner with lava. They undertook some on-task collaboration observed by the researcher but this was not screen captured; the rudimentary model of the eye they produced indicated poor engagement with the learning task.

Leaving aside the anomalous data from the Lava boys, the percentage of on-task behaviour in the screen capture video indicated that groups averaged 65.77% on-task behaviour with 60% of groups being on-task at least 65% of the time (almost half of the groups were on-task 80% or more of the time). Reiterating the need to treat this data as an imperfect window into natural learning behaviour in iVR, we offer two further observations. Firstly, even when students were off-task they were communicating, collaborating, problem-solving, and creating things together in Minecraft VR. They were enacting 21st century skills but did not direct these towards formal learning. Secondly, simply being on-task does not necessarily produce the type of Deeper Learning outcomes (Noguera, Darling-Hammond, and Friedlaender, 2015) that the curriculum requires. Students can be on-task doing 'busy' work that does not develop key skills. Hence, the need to examine learning behaviour within virtual environments.

At this point of this chapter, it is worth recapping the findings of the study reported so far. These were that students in the VR class learnt as much content knowledge (facts and concepts) as their non-VR peers even though they had less traditional explicit (didactic) instructional lesson time and were given an additional six lessons with limited time in iVR to complete an extra, collaborative, higher order learning task using a new technology. The screen capture video data, despite its limitations, indicated that most students were on-task most of the time even though there was variation between groups. The next two sections of this chapter provide a nuanced examination of time-on-task behaviour with a focus on how students regulated their learning behaviour in the virtual environment of Minecraft, with a 'best case' example that resonates with the Deeper Learning framework.

The Regulation of Learning in iVR

Metacognition means 'thinking about thinking' and in adolescence it manifests itself in being able to acquire new insights into effective strategies for information acquisition and ways to solve problems (Berk, 2006). Metacognitive knowledge, or thinking about the skills and strategies for a task and knowing how to apply these and under what conditions, is essential for effective learning (Woolfolk and Margetts, 2010). Metacognition is closely associated with the regulation of thinking which leads to planning, monitoring, and evaluation of action (Berk, 2006). Regulation of learning behaviour is important because when it is effectively taught and learnt in school there is a positive effect on student learning outcomes and achievement (Perry, Lundie, and Golder, 2019).

The screen capture video of on-task activity indicated that students were regulating their learning even though they were not explicitly taught how to do this during the unit of work. The screen capture video included students talking together about what they were doing in VR and non-verbal action where students went about working together on their model. The reasonable amount of non-verbal data collected necessitated the use of a validated theoretical framework that could be sensibly deployed as an observation schedule to code on-task data for regulation. Malmberg, Järvelä, and Järvenoja (2017) developed a dual model for understanding the regulation of learning at both individual and group levels. It should be noted that we did not replicate their temporal and sequential method of analysis. Rather, in this study, we preferred an exploratory approach to understanding patterns of regulation of learning as they naturally occurred in iVR. The first framework from Malmberg et al. (2017) categorises the *processes* of regulation and their empirical indicators. Table 6.5 provides an explanation of these processes with examples from the iVR data.

The on-task screen capture video of students working in their assigned group (10:06:14) was coded according to the process categories outlined in Table 6.5. Only data of students working in their assigned group was coded because we assumed that each group had collectively formed, at the very least, a rudimentary plan of action for the model task (planning, monitoring, and evaluation being the hallmarks of metacognitive regulation), whereas students who were simply assisting another group in an ad hoc fashion would not necessarily be aware of this plan.

Table 6.6 illustrates the wide range of behaviours between groups and overall patterns of regulatory behaviours in iVR. Understandably, given the inextricable link between being on-task and regulating action to achieve a goal, executive function was the most common behaviour. This involved students going about their work in VR by making decisions about the task and assisting group members to undertake relevant activities to build the model. The second most prevalent type of regulatory behaviour was the core metacognitive skills of monitoring and evaluating learning activity followed by planning and task understanding or developing comprehension of the task. That planning and strategy use were least evident was not surprising because students did the majority of their planning and strategising outside of Minecraft VR. The relative scarcity of equipment and VR time meant that learners needed to have contemplated their group's approach to the task, planned and undertaken their research on the body organ, and prototyped their model in desktop or screen mode to import in to Minecraft VR. Consequently, when in Minecraft VR students generally concentrated on collaboratively executing the task through further prototyping and experimenting with the affordances of the medium, and monitoring and evaluating their progress.

The second theoretical framework from Malmberg et al. (2017) categorises types of regulation, with a focus on the social dynamics of learning. Collaborative learning entails self-regulation and regulation as a shared activity. As Malmberg et al. (2017) point out this requires that individuals internalise processes of metacognition, such as monitoring and evaluation, and that these are explicitly shared between group members to ensure joint responsibility for timely, quality task

TABLE 6.5 Categories for regulation processes from Malmberg et al. (2017) with examples from student data

Category	Empirical indicator abridged from Malmberg et al. (2017)	Example from iVR student data
Executive process: Task execution	The group works on and progresses the plan each doing agreed tasks.	*Verbal*: Students work together to clarify and complete parts of the task by discussing the knowledge of the anatomical part and working together to build and fix mistakes e.g. students working together on a model using red blocks. Girl 1: Oh darn [accidentally deleted a block] Girl 2: I'll fix it? Girl 1: Yeah the red wall Girl 2: Okay Girl 1: Oh I got it [fixes it] *Non-verbal*: Students silently work together to build model occasionally looking at the progress of other group members as they undertake the task and assisting by adding a block or two.
Regulation process: Task understanding	Activating previous knowledge of the task and contents; thinking about the purpose of the task; identifying what should be learned; reading and interpreting task instructions; and thinking about why task completion is important.	*Verbal*: Students seek clarification of task. For example, a group have just cleared the field and are about to begin building their model. Girl: So are we making a heart? Boy: No, we are making an eye. Girl: An eye … *Non-verbal*: Students spend time playing with the inventory, tools, and engineering properties of Minecraft to gain technical competency and understanding of its possibilities.
Regulation process: Planning	Thinking about what resources are needed during the lessons and about the relevant parts of a lesson.	*Verbal*: Students discuss what types of blocks in Minecraft to best represent specific parts of a body organ. *Non-verbal*: Students work together to try different types of blocks and engineering properties to create interactive or animated aspects to the model.

(Continued)

TABLE 6.5 (Cont.)

Category	Empirical indicator abridged from Malmberg et al. (2017)	Example from iVR student data
Regulation process: Goal setting	The group sets a goal for the work to be done and sets task-specific goals.	*Verbal*: Student tells group members that they need to collect certain resources from Minecraft to engineer aspects of their model.
Regulation process: Monitoring and evaluating	Monitoring and evaluating progress towards the criteria set for the task; evaluating the time schedule for collaborative tasks; summarising what has been done/needs to be done; and understanding resource availability.	*Verbal:* Students work together on their nearly completed model and one student praises the other student on their work and assesses the work before adding 'What do you think we can add (to the model)?' *Non-verbal*: Student flies through model stopping to assess how it looks and zooming in to take a closer look at certain parts.
Regulation process: Strategy use	Prompting or using the strategy, such as summarising or elaborating on information.	*Verbal*: One student realises a quicker way of making torches to illuminate the interior of a model and says, 'Okay guys, to make torches we can also use charcoal instead of using wood'. *Non-verbal:* Student flicks through the Minecraft inventory of materials and tools trying out some different types of blocks to determine appropriateness for the task.

completion. Table 6.7 presents Malmberg et al.'s (2017) types of regulation – self-regulation, co-regulation, and socially shared regulation – with general empirical descriptors and examples specific to the iVR data.

Table 6.8 indicates that the majority of groups enacted self-regulation and socially shared regulation. Self-regulation was particularly evident in the way individual students 'self-talked' out loud when evaluating, problem-solving, and affirming progress or design decisions. Socially shared regulation indicative of highly developed collaborative dynamics was also common with only two groups showing no evidence of this (although it is likely that we did not screen capture the behaviour). A prominent pattern across groups is the relative lack of co-regulation. Co-regulation is the temporary sharing of regulatory processes between a learner and a more capable other, most often with a teacher facilitating this but sometimes with a peer (Hardwin and Oshige, 2011). In other words, most

TABLE 6.6 Percentage of time on regulation processes by student group*

Group	Task execution	Task under-standing	Planning	Goal setting	Monitoring and evaluating	Strategy use
Eye 1	91.5%	0.0%	0.0%	0.0%	8.5%	0.0%
Eye 2	92.0%	0.0%	0.0%	0.0%	8.0%	0.0%
Eye 3	54.8%	0.0%	0.0%	0.0%	45.2%	0.0%
Eye 4	82.6%	5.0%	5.4%	0.0%	3.1%	3.9%
Eye 5	65.4%	10.7%	15.4%	0.7%	8.7%	3.1%
Eye 6	81.2%	0.0%	0.0%	0.0%	18.8%	0.0%
Artery	86.3%	0.0%	0.0%	0.0%	13.7%	0.0%
Vein/ Artery	100.0%	0.0%	0.0%	0.0%	0.0%	0.0%
Brain 1	80.8%	1.3%	6.3%	0.0%	7.9%	6.5%
Brain 2	88.7%	2.4%	1.9%	0.0%	9.2%	1.0%
Skin 1	57.0%	16.6%	12.7%	0.0%	13.9%	0.0%
Skin 2	75.9%	4.9%	0.0%	0.0%	19.5%	0.0%
Stomach	100%	0.0%	0.0%	0.0%	13.6%	0.0%
Tongue	80.1%	9.4%	4.4%	1.2%	4.0%	0.9%
Heart	68.4%	0.0%	0.0%	0.0%	20.0%	0.0%

* May not add to 100% as segments of screen capture video had minor overlapping regulatory categories or segments were not coded as agreement could not be reached on correct code.

regulation of learning did not involve overt scaffolding between students. Nor were students inclined to tell each other what to do or to simply go along with what was happening in a non-committal way. Relatedly, there was very little 'bossing each other around' conduct evident in the video. Rather, students were much more likely to display individualised or collectively shared regulation as a means towards completing the learning task. This pattern holds even though there is wide variation in the amount of video time we managed to record for each group.

It should be remembered that students did not receive any explicit instruction or scaffolding regarding metacognitive strategies, regulatory behaviour, or collaborative learning as part of the unit of work. Despite this, and keeping in mind the limitations of the data coverage, most exhibited metacognitive processes and positive examples of regulation for learning, especially socially shared regulation as they collaborated in the sandbox environment of Minecraft VR. This indicates that when students were on-task they were not just doing 'busy' work but were clearly engaged on the goal of getting the model built both at individual and group level. In the next section of this chapter we take a dive into Deeper Learning (Noguera, Darling-Hammond, and Friedlaender, 2015) by providing a qualitative case of one of the best examples of collaborative learning through iVR with insights from students on how the affordances of the technology engaged them in the task.

TABLE 6.7 Categories for types of regulation from Malmberg et al. (2017) with examples from student data

Regulation type	Empirical indicator abridged from Malmberg et al. (2017)	Example from iVR data
Self-regulation	A person identifies something they need to do or have done, or what they do not understand. Clear emphasis on the word 'I'.	Student speaking out loud to self says, 'I'll do that'. They then silently execute the task by placing blocks in the structure. Student talks to self while building model and, looking at the placement of blocks says, 'Is that right?' Fixes the block and looks at it from different angles to assess.
Co-regulation	Group members prompt other members to contribute to collaborative group work. Group members explain how they think the group should work and other group members agree and do not add anything new to conversation.	Students work together on their nearly completed model and one student assessing the work says 'What do you think we can add?' Another student looks at model and says, 'Good job'. Student asks group members a series of questions about replacing certain type of building blocks and other features in the model. The response to the series of questions is 'Yeah okay'.
Socially shared regulation	Group members explain how they think the work should proceed. Other group members agree, but they also complement and bring new or additional information to the conversation.	Students work together to make the framework for the model by placing blocks of certain colours in a formation. The conversation goes: *Student 1*: Nah, yeah yeah. I got this. It has to be symmetrical. *Student 2*: We will make it symmetrical. They continue to work together quietly on the framework. The conversation resumes: *Student 1*: There we go. Is that symmetrical? *Student 1*: Yeah. *Student 2*: Wait, no it's not. *Student 1*: Down the bottom there needs to be two. Take that out. They work together to remove the block while the third student looks on to assess that it is even.

TABLE 6.8 Percentage of time by regulation type and student group*

Group	Self-regulation	Co-regulation	Socially shared regulation
Eye 1	57.0%	0.0%	43.0%
Eye 2	23.2%	0.0%	76.8%
Eye 3	73.4%	0.0%	26.6%
Eye 4	22.0%	0.7%	77.3%
Eye 5	41.4%	6.2%	52.4%
Eye 6	85.8%	0.0%	14.2%
Artery	45.5%	0.0%	54.5%
Vein/Artery	100.0%	0.0%	0.0%
Brain 1	22.7%	1.6%	75.7%
Brain 2	69.7%	1.5%	28.8%
Skin 1	57.9%	4.8%	37.3%
Skin 2	44.4%	2.1%	53.5%
Stomach	100.0%	0.0%	0.0%
Tongue	45.6%	11.8%	38.0%
Heart	65.4%	0.0%	22.9%

*May not add to 100% because it was difficult to hear dialogue or there was no dialogue and agreement on code categorisation could not be reached.

'A Skyscraper of a Brain': Student Perspectives on Learning Through iVR

Providing an in-depth case study is an appropriate way to flesh out how the learning affordances of iVR were understood and harnessed by students during the formative assessment task. We operationalise the Deeper Learning framework (Noguera, Darling-Hammond, and Friedlaender, 2015) to consider how the VR task allowed one group of students to exceed learning objectives. To recap, Deeper Learning is evident when students develop content mastery, effective communication, critical thinking and problem-solving skills, collaboration, self-directed learning (akin to metacognition and regulation), and an academic mindset related to a sense of belonging, curiosity, and persistence.

There were a number of exemplary cases from the study to choose from including Eyes 2 and 6, the Vein/Artery, Skin 1 and the Heart. The case study that has been selected is Brain 1 (Figure 6.2) because, in the parlance of the Deeper Learning framework, it represented a comprehensive illustration of how a metacognitive and collaborative approach to learning can lead students to explore and leverage the learning affordance of iVR to demonstrate content mastery and an academic mind set.

FIGURE 6.2 Screenshot looking at night with light blocks symbolising thoughts emitting from brain

The model the boys developed was certainly something to behold and interact with in VR. The boys meticulously researched the brain and nervous system to develop an intricate, engineered model. It consisted of a brain sitting atop a spinal column. The spinal column encased spinal fluid and had representations of ribs and nerve ending extending from it. The boys cleverly designed the brain in two halves. One half was transparent to show how parts of the brain, such as neurons, functioned. In the transparent half of the brain, students used the engineering properties of Minecraft to create a symbolic representation of neurons firing by adding a 'T flip flop' circuit on the spine that could be turned on and off. In their own words, this 'represented stimuli' which activated impulses of the neurons represented and powered by an electrical dust called 'redstone' which was regulated by 'repeaters' (the twin torch like material) (Figure 6.3).

The other half of the brain was solid (Figure 6.4) and had parts that were activated by redstone. Light cubes floated outside the brain to illuminate the model at night (Figure 6.2). The lights also represented thoughts emitting from the brain. The medulla was represented through the use of a textured wool Minecraft block, an idea inspired by an observation made during an animal brain dissection in a lab component of the unit of work.

The guided tour started on the ground at the base of the spinal column where there was a key or legend specifying which types of Minecraft materials were used to represent which parts of the brain. The learner-tourist would then fly up beside the spinal column to view the spinal fluid inside it and they could turn on the 'flip flop' switch to see the neurons firing. Continuing upward, the whole model could be circumnavigated through flight and it was possible to go inside the brain with the guide to experience, up-close, the neurons firing.

In front of both the transparent and solid halves of the brain floated viewing platforms so that if an avatar grew weary of flying, it could rest and take in a view of the model. The model was more than 40 metres high in VR (Figure 6.5). The sheer scale, interactivity, and complexity of the model led the research team to describe it as a 'skyscraper of a brain'.

During the guided tour, the boys articulated comprehensive, factual explanations for parts and functions of the brain and spine *from memory*. They did this unaided by notes or annotations except for the simple legend at the model's base. When asked questions about the brain their responses indicated a high degree of what the Deeper Learning framework calls *content mastery*. This is exemplified in the following transcribed extract from the screen capture video:

STUDENT 1: So on the side of the spinal cord we have some of our nerve endings. Normally these would go on to other parts of the body like the heart and lungs, and if we move up a bit further we have got our ribs and they come up out the side of the back and they would be connected at the front by the sternum, obviously.

STUDENT 3: Then there is the front side of the brain with the nerves and stuff ... if you press the button [on the spine] the lights [in the brain] go on and off.

TEACHER: So what's that meant to represent?

STUDENT 3: The nerves in the brain. Go around the other side of it and see what's inside it. [Go to] the see-through bit.

STUDENT 1: We wanted to use redstone in our brain to represent the way that ... nerves send signals out to the rest of the body ...

RESEARCHER: So what does the brain do?

STUDENT 1: The brain is pretty much the central hub that controls the body. So, stimuli from the environment filters through the brain to help our bodies out in appropriate ways. Say we get scared, our brain immediately sends us into ... the flight or fright ... actions ... Here is some of the spinal juice [fluid] here going up the central column ... of the spine.

RESEARCHER: What does that do?

STUDENT 2: It really protected the nerves and the bone protects it [the nerves] from hits and stuff like if you get hit in the back ... it's protected by that gloop [spinal fluid] ...

STUDENT 1: ... Then we learnt about the oblongata medulla [in a dissection lab].

RESEARCHER: So is the medulla represented in the brain?

STUDENT 2: Yep. So [it is] the pink wool bit.

RESEARCHER: What does the medulla do?

STUDENT 1: It's kinda like for balance, walking, so kinda day-to-day things that we don't think about ...

TEACHER: Like breathing ...

STUDENT 2: When we dissected the brain we saw the wrinkles in the medulla and we thought we could represent that pretty well using wool [blocks] because it's pretty wrinkled like the medulla.

FIGURE 6.3 Screenshot close up of transparent side of brain with redstone electrical dust on blocks activating neurons

FIGURE 6.4 Screenshot of the sold half of the brain with wrinkled 'wool' blocks representing the medulla region

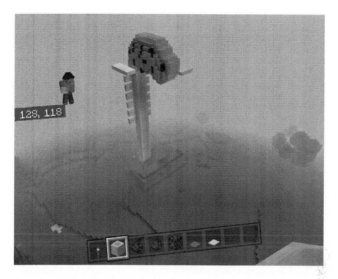

FIGURE 6.5 Daytime screenshot that shows the scale of the brain

During a group interview held after the guided tour, students reflected on the development of other Deeper Learning skills such as collaboration, effective communication, and problem-solving attributing these particularly to the VR component of their learning. The following excerpt from the interview illustrates this:

STUDENT 1: I've learnt a lot in this VR project but it's also made it much more engaging then writing notes down in a book. It makes you want to connect more with the learning that you are doing.

RESEARCHER: So you only had [Minecraft] blocks to build with. What did you think of that?

STUDENT 1: ... Blocks don't really limit you. It just makes you think about it in a more creative way. So instead of making just spherical shapes you have to think about it more to get curves and stuff. Scale is a pretty big thing ... so you need to build at an appropriate scale.

RESEARCHER: Did you have to do a lot of problem-solving, since we're talking about that?

STUDENT 2: The first time we constructed the brain it was very small, low.

STUDENT 1: The first time we constructed the brain [and saw it in VR] the front part was ... pretty much down to the third row of the spinal [cord] and we thought that was really funny. And then we had to go back and fix it up ... We pretty much got rid of the whole thing and then rebuilt the shape to make it look like the brain.

STUDENT 2: We made an outline first before we built it ... by putting the blocks on the edge ... to make a decision on how it looked.

RESEARCHER: How did you make decisions in your group?

STUDENT 1: One of us put up an idea and then we'd all talk about it ... I would most likely try to show an example of what our ideas would look like and then we would all agree on that and then if that didn't look right, like the first time we built the brain, we go back [and] help each other out and try to adapt what we built to out idea.

TEACHER: What would you say was the most difficult part?

STUDENT 2: Originally we had water going down the spine [as spinal fluid]. The water [blocks] soaked everywhere ... and so we got rid of the water entirely and [replaced] it with glass [blocks].

RESEARCHER: What would you say to other students about learning in VR?

STUDENT 1: Well, VR is a very immersive experience. And I feel like if you really take a liking to it, it can be a very useful tool when learning content because it's just not sitting down making you write words. It makes you actually interact with the things you are learning about.

STUDENT 2: It makes you want to go further with it ...

STUDENT 1: It makes you want to keep building, keep making your ideas physical with VR ... You can actually see it right before your eyes ... And it makes you feel like you've done something amazing at the end of it. Just being able to see this brain and all the work we put into it in front of our very own eyes.

RESEARCHER: There were a lot of technical issues with this project. You weren't worried about those? You weren't demotivated?

STUDENT 1: ... the love for the VR project really just wanted us to keep trying to do stuff. When we first started we had a lot of issues with the accounts and the Worlds [referring to networking of Minecraft from the mobile device to the Oculus Rifts]. But we kept trying to find ways to fix it. And I feel like it was all worth it at the end because we figured it out and we built this brain.

STUDENT 2: Yeah and it looks really cool.

The boys' perspective on their persistence in the face of technical and design set-backs and their collective commitment to solving problems as they arose point to the development of an academic mindset. Their positive experience of collaboration is reflected in the almost two hours of screen capture video on the Brain 1 group. It showed they were on-task 87% of the time and that 80% of this was spent diligently progressing their plan for the model with the rest of the time mainly spent on planning, monitoring and evaluating, and strategising. The highly collaborative nature of their approach was reflected in the amount of time they enacted socially shared regulation (75.7%). The self-directed nature of their learning was apparent in their individual ability to self-regulate with this accounting for the remaining 22.7% of time on-task.

The group's appraisal of what iVR bought to their learning highlighted the embodied nature of interaction. Learning in iVR was considered 'more engaging then writing notes down in a book', making students want 'to connect more with the learning' in a 'creative' way. The boys emphasised that instead of 'sitting down writing words' they were actively 'interacting with the things [they were] learning about'. Minecraft allowed them to manifest their ideas in a 'physical' way so that they could see abstract research on the complexity of the brain's structure and function come to life 'right before [their] eyes'. To have their intensive research, planning and prototyping work, and constant difficult problem-solving result in an interactive model that could be fully experienced – from the inside and outside, from the ground to the sky – made them 'want to go further' with their learning.

The immense pride the boys displayed in their model when they gave the researcher a guided tour of it was heartening to see. Boys who were not usually the shining lights of science class had come into their own by learning through iVR.

The Pedagogy of Highly iVR and Teacher Reflections on Student Learning

To begin, it is worth noting that pedagogically, the teachers had cleverly utilised a signature instructional approach of science – the use of representational models to teach about physical and conceptual aspects of phenomena – as the basis for the formative iVR assessment task. This leveraging of a signature pedagogy (Shulman, 2005) of science teaching meant that students were relatively familiar with a variety of biological models, from static to interactive physical 3D models and cross-sections. This allowed students to draw on their prior knowledge of biological models in novel ways. Relatedly, students drew on what they had learnt through participation in the other signature pedagogy of science teaching, laboratory work, to understand how models could represent both interior and exterior aspects of phenomena, in this case body organs. This resonated with the interactive affordances of iVR where the majority of students created models that could be explored inside and outside with many creating accurate internal representations of the body organ (only one group built a cross-section which could not be explored internally but was nevertheless an incredibly detailed and extremely large representation of layers of the skin). Students had dissected a bull's eye in the lab and this influenced the direction of some groups with the eye being a popular model choice (although you could manipulate the scale of it or ride a roller coaster through it or fly right into its lens or splash around in the intraocular fluid of the eye in VR). Furthermore, some groups incorporated ways that the learner-tourist could have some autonomy of interaction over specific aspects of the model by pressing levers or buttons, this being similar to real-life models that can be pulled apart or that have interactive components.

One of the most important pedagogical lessons of the project was how both students and teachers leveraged the signature pedagogy of science through the iVR task building on prior knowledge to extend learning in an experimental and creative realm. During an interview conducted on the final day of the study, one teacher noted that participation in the study had allowed him to redesign and be more flexible with curriculum:

> It has you think about your pedagogy in a different way and how you can redesign your curriculum, redesign your topics and, I guess, being flexible is a part of being a teacher, and it allows you to become more flexible and not getting too hung up on ticking off every single little outcome that might be in the [curriculum] program in any particular order … [It allowed] students to take on paths that they are most interested in and they learn that in a deeper, more rich way.

Reflecting on the learning implications of embedding iVR into science classrooms, teachers noted both the novelty and fun aspect and how some students had exceeded the learning expectations for their current curriculum stage. They described the exceptional mastery of content knowledge, self-direct nature of the learning, development of collaboration and research skills, and the ability of students to be able to authentically communicate their learning beyond the school gate:

RESEARCHER: I was wondering if you could reflect on that [the VR journey]?

TEACHER 1: When I reflect and think back it's just how collaborative it was in terms of what the students would actually do … Giving the students that access [to iVR] is far more valuable. That's going to be something that these kids and these classes is going to remember for the rest of their lives. These are the experiences when you go, 'Do you remember school? Do you remember crazy Mr X and those virtual headsets. How vintage were they.' This is what these kids are going to remember.

RESEARCHER: We've just come out of seeing the kids take us on a tour of the body organ they built and we've had some pretty impressive examples I suppose with kids narrating the tour without notes, without any aids except the annotations [on the organ].

TEACHER 1: It's incredible. That's all you can say. They are talking at levels that are far beyond … the Stage 5 syllabus [the expected junior school curriculum level], their understanding of it. The fact there were no notes [used during the guided tour] really showed not only do they have deep learning, but throughout the process where they have collaboratively problem-solved, they actually are having to have discussions where they have taught each other or they've decided on certain [Minecraft] blocks because of function and property. As a teacher that's one of those fuzzy feelings that gets you through some of the more difficult times in your job because these kids got this [learning] experience and they are taking that away. They will be able to communicate that to other people in the outside world which is ultimately the main goal.

TEACHER 2: In Year 11 and Year 12 [senior school] biology when you are really trying to extend the top kids regarding structure and function [of body organs] and to see Year 9 [junior school] students demonstrate the link between the structure and the function of body organs is pretty amazing. And, the fact that they've created this [model] themselves and ... also the research to build the [model], to get to that point where they can discuss, to whoever is listening, what the parts of the [model] they have built are, what the individual function of those pieces are, and overall what the ... body organ does.

Despite the technically 'arduous' nature of the VR School Study at Callaghan College, the teachers did succeed in developing a unit of work that pedagogically leveraged the signature pedagogies of science teaching for Deeper Learning through iVR for the vast majority of students. Unlike traditional science classes where students are closely supervised and where traditional didactic instruction is common, the teachers took a pedagogical risk in structuring a unit of work to include more self-directed learning and time for a difficult non-graded task to be undertaken in an exciting, relatively unsupervised, and not altogether technically reliable virtual learning environment. This pedagogical risk highlighted the potential for using a sandbox iVR as a holistic environment in which students could demonstrate content mastery through a creative process where problem-solving and authentic communication were key. Ideally students would have had more time, equipment, a more stable technical set up, and instruction and scaffolding to develop collaborative and metacognitive skills. Despite these limitations, teachers suggested that the emphasis on learner autonomy did allow many 'students to take on paths that they (were) most interested in' and this created conditions for them to learn 'in a deeper, more rich way'.

Conclusion

Findings from the Callaghan study have provided some answers to two core questions in iVR educational research: (1) Why use iVR for high school science? and (2) What happens when students undertake a self-directed learning task in an iVR environment that offers an abundance of learning affordances and potential distractions?

To respond, both students and teachers recognised that Minecraft VR provided a broad range of affordances for learning such as: a tool kit to build and engineer a model that could defy real-life scale and allow for an embodied experience of internal as well as external structures; allowing for engaging ways to symbolise biological structure and function through different modes of interaction between learners and the model; and by offering a multi-user environment in which students could learn and work together to accomplish the task. Students could reify the abstract and unseen (neurons firing, the directional flow of blood through the heart, the splash of gastric juices in the stomach, or wading through ocular fluid) and have others experience this by travelling inside the model to see, hear, and interact with the body organ.

Learning in Minecraft VR was facilitated by a visceral connection between learner-environment-model and affordance-action-sociality (see Voulgari and Komis (2012) for a similar analysis of massively multiplayer online games). Simply put, motivated students could actively learn because Minecraft VR provided them with the ability to respond to each other through talk and doing, practice and experimentation, and perspective taking (students built their model with an eye to viewing it down-low, up-high, close up and from afar, and inside and out). As the boys who made the 'skyscraper of a brain' elegantly posited, there is extraordinary power in having to translate the dry facts of science gleaned from a whiteboard or a screen into a fully interactive creation that you have created 'in front of [your] very own eyes', especially when others can enjoy and learn from it. Although virtual objects are not actually 'physical' as the boys suggest, they can be experienced with a sense of perceptual materiality that makes building and experiencing them more engaging and valuable for learning than just 'writing notes down in a book'.

The excitement and higher order thinking that is involved in (re)presenting research through thoughtful creative endeavour is not often a part of high school science classes. Immersive sandbox environments offer a valuable option for leveraging and broadening the signature pedagogies of science education. As the pre- and post-content test results indicate, it is possible, with just a few extra hours added on, to allow for autonomy in learning that combined science with creativity with new technology, and still maintain knowledge acquisition at the same level as that delivered via a traditional didactic pedagogical approach.

In response to the second question – 'What happens when students undertake a self-directed learning task in an iVR environment that offers an abundance of learning affordances and potential distractions?' – the answer is intriguingly multifaceted. Although the screen capture methodology yielded imperfect coverage of group activity in Minecraft VR, the analysis offered a window into the types of student activity and behaviours that teachers might expect when students conduct autonomous learning in a relatively unsupervised (and wondrous) immersive virtual world. While the screen capture we managed to record showed wide variation in the time groups spent on-task, the majority of groups were on-task most of the time and almost half the groups were on-task 80% or more of the time. There is no doubt Minecraft VR proved too distracting for a minority of students and the inability of the teacher to directly supervise activity in the virtual world as they would a real classroom meant that these students were able to maintain off-task behaviour. While this minority of students did not put significant time and attention towards building a body organ model, they were still collaborating, communicating, and regulating their behaviour towards creating other structures in Minecraft VR and working together to destroy these. Redirecting this energy and skill towards the learning task remains a pedagogical challenge, although the students may have been more inclined to take the model task more seriously if it had been graded and the teacher was able to provide more feedback in iVR at different stages of model development. Systematically developing metacognitive and regulatory behaviour in students as part of curriculum would go some way to addressing the need for teacher supervision in VR. However, the fact remains that some students do need consistent supervision and that teachers are unable to spend significant amounts of time in iVR because they still need to supervise and teach in the real world.

The on-task learning that was videoed showed a high degree of goal-directed talk and action with metacognitive behaviour such as planning, monitoring, and evaluation also common across groups. Self-regulation and socially shared regulation were the most common types of regulatory processes with very little co-regulation evident. Self-regulated behaviour is akin to self-directed learning, a core characteristic of Deeper Learning. The frequency of social-shared regulation across groups attests to the highly collaborative nature of much of the student activity that was videoed and observed. Sustained collaboration and communication are also characteristics of Deeper Learning (Noguera, Darling-Hammond, and Friedlaender, 2015). Despite the fact that metacognitive and collaborative skills were not explicitly taught as part of the unit of work, students exhibited these partially as a result of working on a task that gave them autonomy over their learning in a virtual environment with the affordances that allowed them to work together to create amazing interactive models to be enjoyed by other people (or an authentic audience).

The study demonstrated both the difficulties and the delights of embedding an emerging immersive technology into a real classroom in a way that aligned with curriculum and stretched the pedagogical possibilities of science education. The study was premised on the notion that students should be 'active agents who strive to take control of their learning' within a context where learning is influenced by individual and social factors (Hardwin and Oshige, 2011, p. 233). In this research, both the real and the virtual contexts of learning matter a great deal: The preponderance of lab-based studies in the field of iVR and education have led to important influences on learning being largely ignored. The real context of this study was one of a low-income school community that had a depth of teacher expertise but which lacked the material resources of wealthier school communities, and where an achievement gap in learning was evident. This context created a high-stakes environment in embedding an emerging technology in the classroom as we did not want adversely affect the learning outcome of student content acquisition. The virtual context, Minecraft VR, provided an environment that offered an abundance of affordances that allowed students to demonstrate content mastery and other facets of Deeper Learning in a rich and joyous way. Harnessing student enthusiasm for creative, collaborative endeavour for science education can be a challenge; however, as the students of Callaghan College demonstrated with their iVR projects, it is certainly a goal worth pursuing.

References

Berk, L. E. (2006). *Child development*. Boston: Pearson.

Beserra, V., Nussbaum, M., & Oteo, M. (2019). On-task and off-task behavior in the classroom: A study on mathematics learning with educational video games. *Journal of Educational Computing Research*, 56(8), 1361–1383. doi:10.1177%2F0735633117744346

Denzin, N. K. (2012). Triangulation 2.0. *Journal of Mixed Methods Research*, 6(2), 80–88. doi:10.1177/1558689812437186

Godwin, K. E., Almeda, M. V., Seltman, H., Kai, S., Skerbetz, M. D., Baker, R. S., & Fisher, A. V. (2016). Off-task behavior in elementary school children. *Learning and Instruction*, 44, 128–143. doi:10.1016/j.learninstruc.2016.04.003

Hardwin, A., & Oshige, M. (2011). Self-regulation, coregulation, and socially shared regulation: Exploring perspectives of social in self-regulated learning theory. *Teachers College Record*, 113(2), 240–264.

Hunsinger, J., & Krotoski, A. (Eds.) (2013). *Learning and research in virtual worlds*. London and New York: Routledge.

Jensen, L., & Konradsen, F. (2018). A review of the use of virtual reality head-mounted displays in education and training. *Education and Information Technologies*, 23(4), 1515–1529. doi:10.1007/s10639-017-9676-0

Malmberg, J., Järvelä, S., & Järvenoja, H. (2017). Capturing temporal and sequential patterns of self-, co-, and socially shared regulation in the context of collaborative learning. *Contemporary Educational Psychology*, 49, 160–174. doi:10.1016/j.cedpsych.2017.01.009

Noguera, P., Darling-Hammond, L., & Friedlaender, D. (2015). Equal opportunity for Deeper Learning. Jobs for the future. Retrieved https://files.eric.ed.gov/fulltext/ED560802.pdf

NSW Education Standards Authority. (2013). *NSW syllabus for the Australian Curriculum: Science Year 7–10 syllabus*. Sydney: NSW Education Standards Authority.

Perry, J., Lundie, D., & Golder, G. (2019). Metacognition in schools: What does the literature suggest about the effectiveness of teaching metacognition in schools? *Educational Review*, 71(4), 483–500. doi:10.1080/00131911.2018.1441127

Shulman, L. (2005). Signature pedagogies in the professions. *Daedalus*, 134(3), 52–59. https://www.jstor.org/stable/20027998

Sweller, J. (1988). Cognitive load during problem solving: Effects on learning. *Cognitive Science*, 12(2), 257–285. doi:10.1016/0364-0213(88)90023-7

Sweller, J. (2005). Implications of cognitive load theory for multimedia learning. In R. Mayer & R. E. Mayer. (Eds.), *The Cambridge handbook of multimedia learning* (pp. 19–30). Cambridge: Cambridge University Press.

Voulgari, I., & Komis, V. (2012). Antecedents of collaborative learning in massively multiplayer online games. In T. Daradoumis, S. N. Demetriadis, & F. Xhafa (Eds.), *Intelligent adaptation and personalization techniques in computer-supported collaborative learning* (pp. 269–293). Berlin: Springer.

Woolfolk, A., & Margetts, K. (2010). *Educational psychology*. Sydney: Pearson.

7

'BRING WHAT'S GOING ON IN YOUR MIND TO LIFE!'

Using Immersive Virtual Reality in the Drama Classroom

This chapter has been written with contributions by Dungog High School teachers Louise Rowley, Gillian Manning, and David Summers.

Introduction

This chapter is about a high school in a rural, low-income community that took a chance in bringing an emerging technology into the drama classroom. It is a story about a principal who invested precious financial resources in iVR equipment so that a teacher could provide her senior drama class with technology-enhanced learning opportunities not previously available to students. In this case study, we explore how students developed their understanding of the abstract notion of directorial vision by collaboratively exploring the affordances of the sandbox 3D drawing program Tilt Brush to prototype costume and set designs. To tell this story, we draw on qualitative data including: student work samples inside and outside of iVR; video transcripts of student learning inside and outside of iVR; student and teacher focus groups and semi-structured interviews; and teacher written reflections (chapter 4 describes the methodology).

To begin, we describe the study setting, Dungog High School, and its approach to Creative and Performing Arts (CAPA) curricula. We then document the pedagogical approach adopted by the CAPA head teacher in using the virtual design studio of Tilt Brush before exploring the student journey of working inside and outside of iVR to develop sophisticated conceptions of directorial vision realised through symbolic aspects of costume and set design within an immersive environment. We then return to the teacher perspective in order to sum up the main lessons related to using iVR in curriculum-aligned ways in a rural school community.

Setting the Scene

Situated in a rural township, Dungog High School prides itself on connection to its local community and the feeder primary schools that are dotted around the district. The Dungog economy is based on agriculture and timber with the area attracting tourism due to its rugged bush beauty. The school's ethos emphasises building quality relationships within the context of a comprehensive curriculum spanning academic, cultural, sporting, and vocational subjects. Over the last few years, the school has been focused on developing innovative pedagogies to engage students in Science, Technology, Engineering, Arts, and Mathematics (STEAM) as well as improving literacy and numeracy outcomes. Beyond the usual academic competencies, the small Creative and Performing Arts (CAPA) faculty are dedicated to developing student skills in creativity, collaboration, and decision-making. They also seek to build the confidence and self-discipline of students through their learning. The CAPA head teacher and co-researcher on the VR project, Louise Rowley, often talked about the 'Four Cs' – Communication, Collaboration, Creativity, and Critical Reflection – informing her practice.

Like many Australian rural communities, internet access in the Dungog region is variable. In the township and school, access to broadband is reasonable; however, outside of town broadband connectivity, reliability, and speed varies considerably. Dungog High School is a low-income school community (see chapter 4 on this). Some of its students have access to the latest digital devices and data plans that enable extensive online learning while many do not. Some students do not own a smart phone or other mobile device. This makes the school an important hub for digital learning and using technologies for global connection.

Curriculum and Pedagogical Approaches to Harnessing iVR in the Creative Process

Dungog High School's journey into iVR began with a conversation between Erica Southgate and CAPA head teacher Louise Rowley about extending the use of the technology beyond the usual STEM subjects. Erica invited the teacher to come to the university to try out the Oculus Rift and subsequently Erica took the equipment to Dungog High School to allow other teachers and select students to experience iVR. Work then began on developing a project where the technology could be used in a Year 11 (senior) drama class of nine students. During the period in which the idea for the project was germinating the principal of Dungog High School created a scheme where staff could apply for seed funding for innovative teaching and learning projects. The teacher put in an application to use iVR in her CAPA faculty and received enough funding to buy two Oculus Rifts with Touch Controllers, Alienware laptops, a small amount of money for software acquisition, and teacher 'buy-out' time to implement the project with the university researcher.

A team of teachers was formed to run the project. The team comprised CAPA head teacher Louise Rowley who would develop curriculum material and teach the class (hereafter referred to as the teacher), e-Learning coordinator Gillian Manning, and librarian David Summers who provided technical and learning support. The team decided to use Tilt Brush, a 'no code create' 3-D drawing program, because it offered a virtual design studio that would allow students to experiment with and quickly prototype costume and set designs for instant teacher and peer feedback. Tilt Brush is a sandbox type of VR (chapter 3 has a pedagogical typology of iVR). Importantly, it would work offline and so would not take up school bandwidth to run. Unfortunately, being a government school, the internet network blocked the game store and updates. This meant that updates had to be undertaken by teachers who took the equipment home or used data on their personal smart devices to do this at school.

The teacher developed a unit of work based on the contemporary Australian play *Ruby Moon* (Cameron, 2005). The play, which combines absurdist and gothic genres, explores what happens to family and community when a child goes missing. Students would work in groups of three to create a director's folio, traditionally comprising written work on staging the director's vision and demonstrating how this would be reflected in a theatre set box and drawings of costume design. In addition, students would create an immersive experience of their directorial vision in Tilt Brush for others to experience. The learning outcomes, paraphrased from the Board of Studies NSW (2009) Drama Stage 6 Syllabus, were that student should: (1) understand, manage, and manipulate theatrical elements and elements of production, using them perceptively and creatively to explore how an audience might relate to set and costume design; (2) develop their understanding of the contributions to a production of the director and designers to communicate meaning during the theatre experience; and (3) understand the contributions to a production of, among others, the director and designers in using dramatic and theatrical elements to engage an audience (for more on the unit of work see chapter 4). The drama syllabus explicates the overarching intent of learning objectives in the following way:

> In Drama, students can investigate, shape, and symbolically represent ideas, feelings, attitudes, beliefs and their consequences. By studying this major art form students acquire skills in interpretation, communication, performance and critical analysis and become aware of the technical processes and technologies that may be used to heighten dramatic presentation. In the critical study of drama and theatre students can recognise the collaborative contribution of actors, directors, playwrights, designers and technicians to production. (Board of Studies NSW, 2009, p. 5)

The aim of the Dungog High School study was to understand how the affordances of iVR technology could enable students to progress discipline-specific higher order thinking such as symbolic interpretation and manipulation of design elements while also developing collaboration skills. The teacher, who had over two decades of teaching experience, took an open approach to exploring what iVR could offer her students. She researched how theatre companies were using iVR and found that the UK National Theatre had developed an immersive Alice in Wonderland audience experience. The teacher shared this with the students as part of an introductory lesson on the possibilities of the technology for theatre. The teacher included a formative assessment task in the unit of work which utilised Tilt Brush. This task involved students, in their groups, creating an immersive environment in which an audience could experience the mood, atmosphere, and symbols of their directorial vision. This would be reflected in the design of specific elements of set, costume, and other evocative virtual objects. The following videoed exchange between teacher and student captures the intention of the task:

TEACHER: [Talking to a student who is in VR] So what exactly are you doing right now?

ELLE: [While standing and working rapidly on the design in VR] I'm building an interactive space that the audience can come in and experience a piece of our directorial vision more in depth than they would have just having a small experience of just the physical theatre so that they can come in and immerse themselves in an extra space and, oh opps [makes a mistake in VR and quickly fixes it], be more immersed in the theatre process.

The teacher displayed a remarkable openness to exploring the potential of the technology and flexibly weaving its use into the unit of work. For example, the VR learning task was refined as she and the students gained more knowledge of and confidence in using Tilt Brush. In the following written reflection written at the conclusion of the study, the teacher describes an early willingness to 'trust' that the creative process, combined with a fearless readiness to learn *with* students, as guiding her pedagogy in using iVR in the classroom:

> [Using Tilt Brush] was a truly creative process as we really didn't know where we were heading as it was experimental and we were willing to go down this path with a trust in the process. We knew we would find something in the design process but we had to go through the process to find it. This can be quite scary for teachers who often feel they need to know everything before they start. Everything was new though and this allowed us to really share the experimenting and discoveries along the way. Inspiring each other as we discovered the potential of the software and how differently we could create a set design and led us to discover a whole new theatre experience for the audience. This was truly being innovative.

This pedagogic approach is the opposite of 'technicised' notions of pedagogy that frames teaching as the unidirectional transmission of a-priori knowledge and skills from teacher to student. As this reflection demonstrates, the teacher positions her practice with the emerging technology of iVR as a shared experience of discovery. This is what Lusted (1986) means when he talks about pedagogy as transformative practice where knowledge is produced as students and teacher collectively and consciously assert agency over learning through 'thought, discussion, writing, debate, exchange; in the social and internal, collective and isolated struggle for control of understanding; from engagement in the unfamiliar idea, the difficult formulation pressed at the limit of comprehension or energy ...' (p. 4).

As a seasoned educator, the teacher felt confident in trusting that the structure of the unit of work combined with the uncertainties of the creative process would yield good learning outcomes. While there are many ways to conceive of the creative process, it is commonly considered as a series of (intersecting) phases such as: *orientation* where the problem is initially conceived or sensed; *preparation* where work is initiated according to a nascent idea or impression and incubated through illuminating moments and creative gestures (sketches, drafts, mock-ups); and *production* consisting of the realisation of an idea transposed into its final medium which can prompt validation and reflection (Botella, Zenasni, and Lubart, 2018).

The teacher recognised that during the orientation phase students would need to induct themselves into both a theoretical knowledge regarding the affordances of iVR for learning and a technical knowledge of the features of Tilt Brush for creative and collaborative design purposes. Simultaneously they would need to explore how the abstract notion of directorial vision might be reflected in an immersive experience. Moving to the preparation phase, students would be stretching their imaginations and knowledge of the absurdist and gothic genres by prototyping designs using the many features of Tilt Brush such as wide variety of 'brushes' and animations (fire, stars, smoke, and pulsating connectors), existing 3D models in the program, and manipulating the colour and lighting of the atmosphere ('sky box') to create different moods.

During these early phases, in particular, there was the potential for students to experience cognitive overload. Cognitive overload occurs when learners become too distracted to process and retain information resulting in an inability to build a complex understanding of the topic (Sweller, 1988; 2005). The many features of Tilt Brush, the intensity of the immersive experience itself, and the double complexity of translating abstraction through symbolism had the potential to produce cognitive overload (the deleterious effects of this on adults learning through iVR has been documented by Makransky, Terkildsen, and Mayer, 2019). From the beginning and throughout the unit of work, the teacher used a 'guided play' (Weisberg, Hirsh-Pasek, Golinkoff, Kittredge, and Klahr 2016) pedagogical approach, which focused students on how the affordances of iVR could be used to realise directorial vision. This took the form of the teacher questioning individuals and groups at strategic stages of the unit of work and involved the group brainstorming responses to sets of questions intended to prime their imaginations and direct them towards purposeful play. For example, at the beginning of the unit of work, and after only a few familiarisation experiences of iVR (only one student had tried VR before the project), students were asked to brainstorm responses to the following questions:

> Imagine what you can do in VR/Tilt Brush world that you can't do in the real world? What do you think the technology will allow you to do? How do you think these tools may help your learning?

Students' responses to these questions (Figure 7.1) were insightful given their limited experience of the technology:

> With this technology we will be able to step inside the set and act around it. Create things [and] move thing around easier. Play around with scale. Visualise things more easily. It will give us access to things we didn't pay for.
>
> [In VR you can] see your work from every dimension. Get inside your design. You can try things and see how they work.
>
> [In VR] you can bring what's going on in your mind to life. There's a huge open window to what you can do. You can create things that haven't been physically created before [or] things that … couldn't be made into physical reality. Nothing's permanent – you erase all the things you've done with a press of a button – less mess/damage.

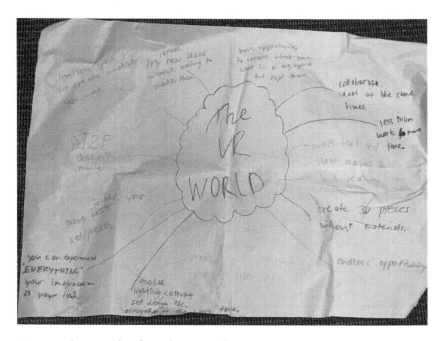

FIGURE 7.1 An example of a student group brainstorm

In the large group discussion that followed this brainstorm activity both teacher and students unpacked how Tilt Brush could enable perspective-taking, ease of proto-typing and experimentation, allow access to materials and effects not available in the classroom, save time during the collaborative process, and allow for the 'snowball' of ideas. This extract of dialogue from the video of the large group discussion illustrates the many ways students thought iVR could assist them with the learning task:

TEACHER: So let's just have a discussion on [those questions and] anyone can jump in and have a bit of a chat about that.

FELIX: Well I sort of relate it … to the real world [and] not just to the drama room, and I said that in VR you can travel to different places around the world and it sort of widens the things you can do. It gives you a lot more options and you can try new things but if you don't like the thing you can then just take it away and clear it [in Tilt Brush].

TEACHER: Do you like that idea Felix?

FELIX: Yes I do. It makes things much easier.

TEACHER: So the editing process is something that's live and reactive and immediate … For example on a set design you might spend weeks and weeks and weeks on creating the actual [set] box or the costume but in VR you can make it and erase it and make it again and change the colour, tone, hue, add light, add fire whatever. It gives you so much more possibility.

KAREN: And with being a school you only have a set budget but when you have [Tilt Brush] you can like 'I want to put this here and this here' so you can create things that your school might not necessarily have the access to but you can create it and say, 'Yeah that works', and if, as you are creating, the ideas sort of snowball on and you get see if I'm in this scene I will be standing here and the light might be more effective if I was standing here and you could physically be inside the set and say, 'Nah that's not working,' and change it.

SALLY: Yeah give you a whole new perspective and what you're doing because you are seeing inside it and outside it as you do it.

TEACHER: And then you can take other people into it. So it's just not you.

SALLY: So it's a new experience.

TEACHER: So there's your audience.

FELIX: Other people can see your imagination.

LANA: Yeah you're not limited to space or size or limited to what you can create. It's like costume and set is all in the one place. You can access it all at the one time which means you have less man work in physically getting the materials, putting them all together, and lining them up perfectly … and you can erase, experiment, and put more things in.

KAREN: It also saves time in that set design, Ok we are going to physically create it, then get this out, do this, do this, every single lesson. VR you just chuck it [the headset] on and then you're in [your design].

TEACHER: How's it going to help your learning?

SALLY: It's going to be easier to get what's in our mind out. Cause, I know, a lot of the time I struggle putting my stuff into words but if I can draw it and just put it out there into art then it's a lot easier for me.

FELIX: And to elaborate on what Karen said before. It takes a lot of time to set up the scene over and over again at the start of each lesson. And the VR [design] it's just there so you'll be able to do more in that lesson and learn more.

KAREN: For learning opportunities, you can create, you can experiment, and you can put other people in there as well and they can help you with ideas. Experiment and play is [what] makes you learn and VR makes that possible.

The teacher used this brainstorming technique at different stages of the unit of work to maintain student focus on what they were learning through iVR. This pre/re-training pedagogic technique (Mayer and Moreno, 2003), where learners are scaffolded towards constructing a mental model of the components to-be-learned or utilised in a digital application, kept students on-task, making it less likely that they would experience cognitive overload. By starting the unit of work with a 'pre-training' exercise and punctuating progression through the unit with activities that required a re-focusing on the learning aspects of using the technology, the teacher encouraged students to go beyond the novelty effect towards a more metacognitive framing of its efficacy for learning. Students were asked to think about how they were thinking about the technology for learning. This stretched them to holistically consider the learning affordances of Tilt Brush, an advance on the simple 'tech-as-tool' approach. For example, when students experimented with changing lighting or importing music into their immersive creations, or when they went into another group's environments, they were asked by the teacher to reflect on how the mood of virtual space was influenced by these elements.

To further mitigate the potential for cognitive overload, the curriculum was sequenced and paced in a cyclical way to ensure a balance of design time outside and inside of VR. Outside of VR, students worked in their groups to develop different aspects of their directorial vision and explore how this might be reflected or symbolised through costume and set design using text, drawing, and collage. This meant that students had nascent design elements that they wanted to recreate and develop in Tilt Brush during the time they had access to it (15 minutes per student per lesson or up to 45 minutes per small group per lesson). They would then experiment in Tilt Brush by changing brushes, adding animations, creating, resizing, and moving virtual objects, viewing them from various distances and angles by teleporting, altering lighting, and taking photos and gifs of their work for later individual and group reflection.

As the unit of work progressed the teacher displayed pedagogical agility in adjusting the expectations of the VR task. As a newcomer to the technology, and with no pedagogical model to guide its use in the drama classroom, the teacher adjusted the task expectation when it became evident that a significant degree of time and technical drawing talent was required to develop fully realised 3D design elements. While some students displayed an aptitude for drawing both in traditional 'pen and paper' mode and in VR, many did not. Although Tilt Brush supplies the tools to manifest a creative vision, a high degree of artistic talent and technical training is required to make fully realised and evocative virtual objects: In other words, Tilt Brush may be a studio with an array of content creation tools but it won't make someone a better artist (hence the need for student engagement with discipline-related knowledge and skills if they are seeking to demonstrate technical accomplishment). In response to the modest artistic skills of most students, the teacher adjusted the expectations of the VR task asking the groups to concentrate on producing an audience experience with just a few well-defined symbolic visual and sound elements which would evoke the mood and atmosphere of their directorial vision.

The flexibility and responsiveness the teacher displayed in adjusting the expectations of the VR task reflected one of the signature pedagogies of drama teaching, improvisation (Davis, 2015). The openness of the creative process to improvisation allowed the teacher to fine-tune the task expectation as the class collectively learnt what was possible and feasible. The task narrowed and shifted to a more process oriented focusing on collaboratively experimenting with symbolism.

At this point of this chapter, it is worth recapping the main findings of the Dungog High School study reported so far. This case study demonstrated that the pedagogical approach to using iVR is most powerful when it aligns or resonates with the signature pedagogies of the discipline of the subject being taught, in this case drama. Furthermore, the study illustrated how the choice of iVR environment can significantly extend on how the subject is ordinarily delivered: In this case, the choice of iVR sandbox environment (Tilt Brush) acted as and provided the tools of a design studio that was more than complementary to the workshop environment of the drama classroom. Tilt Brush offered many more affordances for easy prototyping of an imaginative directorial vision at and beyond scale than the material resources of the real world classroom which conventionally rely on construction of miniature cardboard set boxes for the task.

The following sections of this chapter examine how students developed a deep understanding of how to manifest abstract ideas such as symbolism and affective states such as mood in their immersive directorial vision of the play. The chapter is rounded off with a section highlighting teacher reflections on learning together with students as a key outcome of the project.

Beginning the Learning Journey Through iVR

Most students relished the opportunity to use VR to experiment with their directorial vision: Only one student was reluctant, citing her preference for 2D drawing. The student journey could be characterised as moving from cooperation to collaboration *and* from a relatively surface engagement with the play's absurdist and gothic themes to an in-depth exploration of symbolism related to these genres with an exploration of how this might be experienced by an audience. It is worth unpacking these intersecting trajectories in order to better understand how an iVR application that is not a multi-user environment could be leveraged for collaboration to enable higher order, symbolic thinking.

While the terms cooperation and collaboration are often used interchangeably, they essentially describe two different social processes. Cooperation involves dividing up a task into different parts with each person in a group responsible for working on that part to contribute back to the whole. Collaboration is a collective and coordinated whole group effort in problem-solving and enacting solutions together. Kozar (2010) sums up the differences with cooperation being more product focused with each group member individually doing an assigned task which, when combined, contribute to an end product or goal, while collaboration is an ongoing interactive process where participants share and create knowledge together through negotiation, discussion, perspective-taking, and by accommodating different views in the development of a solution or product.

At the beginning of the unit of work, the teacher noted that student groups were organising themselves according to a cooperative model where members would assign each other specific tasks and do these individually. The gradual move from cooperation to collaboration was facilitated by the teacher who had an early discussion with students about collaborative practice through explorative, playful engagement with the technology. Even though Tilt Brush is not a multi-user environment, the small class size (n=9), large physical space of the classroom (Figure 5.3 in chapter 5), and access to two sets of VR equipment meant that groups of students could cycle in and out of VR rapidly depending on the stage of design. It was common that while one student from the group was in VR experimenting with or creating a design element, other group members would be either standing at the edge of the play area and giving aesthetic and/or technical advice or sitting nearby undertaking 2D design work while also chatting with the student in VR. The following transcribed videoed interaction demonstrates how one student Elle, who is in VR, interacts and collaborates with classmates who are not part of her assigned group but who are standing outside the play area:

ELLE: [Has bought up an existing virtual model of a manikin in Tilt Brush] I could give it [the costume design] a crack [a try]. [She begins to select brushstrokes and paints the manikin].

FELIX: Try to make it [the brush stroke] thicker … I can't remember how I made it thicker. [Elle starts flicking through options on the virtual palate].

ELLE: Whoa [uses the controller joy stick to make the brush thicker and jumps back slightly as she draws a thicker brush stroke]. There we go. So if I made her an electric red dress.

FELIX: Like a dress off [the movie] *The Hunger Games*.

ELLE: Yes it's easier to draw the costume on to the manikin. Oh yes. Let's not do the back yet.

DEE: Can you try to grab it [the manikin 3D model]?

ELLE: So if you grab it at the same time with two hands [she resizes the model as her peers look at the computer screen]. Yes!

Groups of three could have up to 45 minutes to work on their design in VR (individual students were limited to 15 minutes in VR per lesson with no VR allowed if it was the final lesson of the school day). However, it was common for groups to use this time in a non-sequential manner, that is, for students to jump in and out of Tilt Brush to either add to the design or give feedback and suggestions. The fluid interactions inside and outside of VR were a central feature of the creative process: The virtual studio of Tilt Brush and the real studio of the drama room blurring into a collective collaborative space.

Pre-trained and strategically prompted to consider the learning affordances of Tilt Brush, students iterated designs from 2D paper to 3D virtual objects while simultaneously exploring the meaning and power of symbolism. Tilt Brush allowed students to experiment with and fully realise how symbolism might be iterated at and beyond regular scale, something that was impossible to accomplish through traditional 2D 'pen and paper' representations or the production of a miniature cardboard set box. This not only aligned with the curriculum objective of encouraging students to 'investigate, shape, and symbolically represent ideas, feelings, attitudes, beliefs and their consequences' (Board of Studies NSW, 2009, p. 5), but also enhanced exploration and understanding of symbolism related to genre. As elucidated in the following transcribed video excerpt, students experimented with how the play's themes of debilitating grief might be represented in a directorial vision:

TEACHER: So what is the window for?

LANA: [Responding while moving around and working on the design in VR] So this is the basis of our whole project where we are having the nine stages of grief and the window symbolises acceptance and where they [the parent characters of Ruby, the missing child] haven't accepted what's wrong with them. There's a padlock on the window symbolising this. There is a lock on the window because they haven't really accepted Ruby's loss so that's what we are trying to aim for. The window kind of represents like moving forward and opening towards a new horizon but it's locked because [they] are stuck.

In Tilt Brush, the symbolic could manifest before the eyes through fully embodied creative interaction. Using gesture and movement, elements of set and costume design could be bought alive, quickly altered, or refined by changing brushes, adding animation, and resizing the scale of the element. The mood of the design elements could be altered instantly by adjusting lighting or adding music. The virtual studio offered a rich sensory experience of creation. Importantly, by navigating (teleporting) around the Tilt Brush studio, students could get immediate insight into how the audience, actors, or director might experience the symbols and mood of the directorial vision. This generated a visceral sense of the abstract, of how symbolism can profoundly influence a theatrical experience. For example, Lana could effortlessly teleport up to, behind, and away from the virtual window she was creating, thus enhancing her understanding of the symbol from the different perspective of audience, actor, and director. Her group could effortlessly share this experience with other students and the teacher, facilitating ongoing feedback and adjustments to the design. iVR, like some other digital technologies, offered a sense of immediacy in design, a liveliness in real-time interaction with between creator and what is being made, and between the creators, their peers, and the teacher (Davis, 2015). However, unlike 2D design tools, students could literally move around and interact with the symbols from multiple, embodied perspectives.

Students' designs were highly expressive, evolving as the unit of work progressed. For example, one group experimented with a number of elements before settling on building an enormous spider web consisting of black tubes with red flashing animated connectors in which a large shadowy red-back spider (a local venomous species) hung down from the top of the web. Within the web was a golden cage – a trap within a trap. It was possible to teleport inside and around the web and in and around the cage: an ominous experience. The students suggested that the mood of the design would be one of claustrophobia and that it represented both the way the characters in the play were 'stuck in time' because of their loss and grief. They also wryly commented that it symbolised the World Wide Web and was a statement on how society is trapped by technology, an interesting statement given their use of an emerging technology for learning.

Another group explained how they depicted the play's theme of grief through VR. This group included Lana who described making the locked window representing non-acceptance of grief in the quote above. In the following video transcription her peers describe leveraging the seemingly infinite studio space of Tilt Brush to evoke mood:

DEE: Our directorial vision is loss and grief and we are representing this in our VR set through all the stages of grieving. So we are planning on having this big grove.

JASPER: Yes a massive grove.

DEE: With floating pictures of all the stages except acceptance [there is then a discussion with the teacher about representing a lack of acceptance through the symbol of the locked window].

TEACHER: So what do you want your audience to experience when they are in your immersive VR space?

DEE: The isolation of these feelings.

JASPER: The loneliness within that space because it's going to be so massive.

The next section of this chapter provides a detailed examination of how one group developed their immersive directorial vision by iterating 2D design into VR.

An Immersive Fractured Fairy Tale

One of the most evocative and well-considered virtual spaces was created by Felix, Sally, and Elle. This group, consisting of the more reserved students in the class, created their immersive directorial vision through a thoughtful process of investigating the play's themes and iterating symbolic meaning through gothic mood and absurdist style. Their engagement in the play's text was ongoing. During the orientation phase of the creative process they identified key themes, symbols, and character reference points from the play brainstorming how these might be symbolically represented during the preparation via detailed and annotated 2D drawings of costumes and set design: Many of these elements would be eventually expressed in the production of their immersive space. In the early phases, Felix produced detailed sketches of set and costume design based on the group's ideas. The set design (Figure 7.2) emphasised the disintegration of the neighbourhood environment as a parallel to the breakdown of reality for the characters in the play and the uncertainty, for the audience, of who is telling the truth about the child's disappearance. The set design included a large red moon (a play on the missing child's name Ruby Moon), cobwebbed doors, a fireplace that could not possibly

FIGURE 7.2 Early drawing of the set design produced by the fractured fairy tale group

warm a decomposing room, and an ambiguous broken doll that might be the child's toy or representative of Ruby herself. The costume sketch in Figure 7.3 is of the mother Sylvie Moon whose hair mimics that of her lost child and the broken doll in the set design. Here a polka dot scarf also reflects the lost child.

When the group brainstormed the design for their immersive directorial experience they decided to create a fractured fairy tale returning to many of the elements they had already developed in their 2D sketches but also adding other symbols to emphasise the disintegrative mood. Sally explained their vision:

SALLY: Our sort of idea and director's vision is based off a gothic fairy tale. We sorta wanna enhance that idea and make it our own by scattering everything, everywhere. Fracturing everything because we see it as this massive fractured fairy tale that doesn't necessarily make sense. We don't want anything that actual works.

TEACHER: So what do you want the audience to experience once they go inside your VR experience?

SALLY: A disconnect.

FIGURE 7.3 Early costume design drawing for the mother character

As the brainstorm document (Figure 7.4) illustrates, the existing 2D design elements of the moon, the fireplace, the cobwebs, the pig-tailed doll, and a door to nowhere are supplemented with other gothic symbols such as a crow, a scary clown face (one of the play's character's was clown), suspended spirals, body parts, and a polka dot dress reminiscent of the scarf in the costume sketch.

In the following transcribed excerpt from a video of Felix creating part of the directorial vision in VR, the symbolic nature of immersive experience is explained:

TEACHER: What are you doing?

FELIX: [Talking while kneeling on the floor and rapidly creating the design in VR] Right now I'm trying to fill in the empty gaps of the fireplace and I have completed the outline of the door somewhere, oh over here [gesturing towards the virtual door to nowhere which sits by itself away from the fireplace] for someone to complete later. And we are trying to get the sense of it being a gothic fairy tale and of having spooky things everywhere like a body part in one place and a raven in another place.

TEACHER: Ok excellent keep working [Felix goes to build the foundation of the fireplace].

The design utilised a night 'sky box' which made the many elements which were drawn in bright colours or which utilised animations stand out in the darkened space. For example, a roughly drawn faceless doll (Figure 7.5), which was

FIGURE 7.4 Fractured fairytale group's design brainstorm

FIGURE 7.5 The animated doll near the disintegrating fireplace

depicted in the initial set sketch (Figure 7.2), had the child-like pig tails of the mother character (Figure 7.3). It was sitting on the ground, isolated but festooned with fairy lights and lit up with sparking animations emanating around it. The fireplace, transparent in places (a nod to disintegration), had animated fire and a creepy picture of a clown on its mantelpiece. In another part of the space an animated suspended spiral, that changed colours, whirled endlessly giving the impression that it would swallow the spectator. There was also a door to nowhere. A very large blood moon pulsated behind an animated cloudy atmosphere dominating the space just as Ruby Moon's disappearance had come to haunt the lives of the characters in the play. A scrap of red polka dot fabric lay discarded in the foreground of the moon both seemingly insignificant and important in its allusion to the lost child and her mother (Figure 7.6).

It is difficult to capture in words and through still photographs the dynamic mood of the virtual space and the impact of the elements scattered throughout it. This is especially true of the combination of darkened 'sky box', brightly coloured objects, and strategically placed animations which bought the elements alive. While the elements were not always technically perfect, the combination of them, their dynamic nature, and layout evoked a feeling of strange discontinuity. The success of the virtual production in evoking the group's directorial vision was appraised by their classmates who provided the following positive reflections on experiencing it in VR:

TEACHER: What did it feel like to be in there and what did you see?

ANITA: It was very hectic. Because I'd been in VR before, I thought if it was my first time I'd find it very full on because there's a lot going on. It's all very misjointed and it had like an optical illusion [animated spiral] that you couldn't look at for too long. And they had a fire place with like a clown picture on top of it which was creepy. They had a door frame and all this other stuff and it was just really unreal to look at it. There was a lot of different lighting and stuff. It was really cool … I loved it. It was definitely unreal, really good.

JASPER: That VR space was very enjoyable. My favourite part of it was the blood moon that was pulsating with energy. I would never have thought to do that or even conceptualised it with a drawing.

TEACHER: What did you feel while you were in there?

JASPER: Well I felt, what did I feel? … It was, what's the word, intriguing, fascinating? Curious! That's what I felt like.

TEACHER: Did you have any idea what their directorial vision was trying to achieve?

JASPER: Absurdity. You could clearly tell that from the way everything was made. It looked very cartoon like. It was also very twisted. Very gothic. You could tell this from the themes that they used, the colours

TEACHER: So Dee, you just road tested a VR design from another group. So what were your impressions when you were in there?

DEE: It was very absurd like it's supposed to be in the plot [of the play]. Like the door is transparent so you can see outside. This big red moon is in the centre but it's inside the house with the fireplace right beside it.

TEACHER: So how did you feel?

DEE: I didn't know I how I felt. It was like really random … It was the absurdity of a twisted fairy tale.

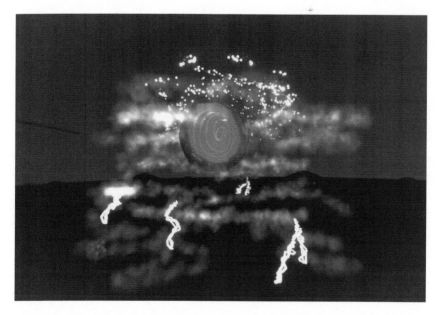

FIGURE 7.6 The ruby-coloured moon with animated atmosphere floating around it and fragment of polka dot fabric in foreground

Tilt Brush provided an immersive studio with a wide array of content creation tools that gave students an opportunity to experiment, prototype, and share a dynamic and interactive version of their directorial vision in a way that was fundamentally different from traditional approaches such as 2D drawings and miniature cardboard set boxes. Even though Tilt Brush was not a multi-user environment it was conducive to collaboration as students could instantly create, share, build on, and get feedback on each other's work as they seamlessly moved between working in 2D to 3D. Importantly, Tilt Brush made it possible to shift between perspectives by teleporting around the virtual objects and viewing these close up as an actor would or at a distance as an audience might. Through perspective-taking, the manipulation of the scale, colour, and dynamism of symbols, lighting effects, and sound, students gained a deeper understanding of the importance of these elements in theatre design. The teacher suggested that this creative experience in Tilt Brush positively influenced the way students approached the creation of their traditional set box and written assessment on directorial vision.

'We Were Thinking Like Directors': Student Reflections on How iVR Enhanced Learning

Students marked the final phase of the creative process, which involves validation and critical reflection, by discussing their experiences in a focus group and in peer-to-peer interviews. In the focus group they discussed their initial feelings of excitement and trepidation coupled with a readiness to play with the technology:

RESEARCHER: What did you think about the very beginning of the VR experience …?

SALLY: I thought it was cool. I freaked out like, you probably remember, it was that interesting. Just a whole new experience from just looking at a [video game] on a phone [screen] to being in it.

KAREN: I remember watching the video that Miss [Rowley] showed us of the man painting the bird [in Tilt Brush] and thinking I'm going to be horrible at this because I can't art whatsoever and like it's going to be cool to be in there but I'm not going to have the same experience as everyone else. But you did. I got in there and you're like I don't care I can only draw a stick man, watch me go [group laughter]. It was like really good.

LANA: Like it brings out your creative side. Like you want to imagine because there's so much you can do with it … Because it's very much about play. Like you go in there with ideas but using just the different tools, different textures, and different colours, and different environments it all just layers on top of each other and it makes it something new …

FELIX: You go in there thinking I know nothing about it but then you just start playing around with things and you figure out stuff really fast and you get good at it.

DEE: ... It was so cool being inside it and once you got the hang of it you could do anything.

ELLE: When I first used it I'd never used anything virtual reality ... so I didn't know how it would turn out. But when I put the headset on it was really different and I got used to it really quickly ...

KAREN: And you saw some people go into it and get lost in it. Like they went in there and like this is amazing. Like you Lana definitely went, 'Like I've got this idea and that idea and let me do this,' and [we're] like, 'Fifteen minutes is up Lana', and you're like, 'Na na na no. I want 20 more minutes. Don't stop [me]'. You saw some people get right into it and really love it ...

CHRIS: It was like is this going to be just us mucking around or will it be worthwhile doing it in class ...

Students linked the playfulness of the virtual environment to its affordances which complemented the formative assessment task and enabled learning. They contrasted the traditional approach to set and costume design with the unique design features of Tilt Brush such as the array of drawing tools that are not available in the real world and the ability to experiment with these and easily correct mistakes. They thought that actually 'being inside' a space with costume and set elements, at and beyond scale, provided them with a better sense of 'all the different things [they could] accomplish':

RESEARCHER: So what do you think you could do in there that was different from your other work in drama?

LANA: Apart from being inside it? [The class laughs]. Well I like to do the traditional stuff. Draw it before you go in. But then you get to mess around with the colours, the height, the textures of the set design that's around you. You can play with the texture of the floor.

SALLY: I think the best part is if you make a mistake you just press undo.

CHRIS: It's like writing an essay on a computer is a lot more easier than writing it on a page cause a mistake you're not scribbling it out. It's basically like that but art.

KAREN: That is such a good analogy.

LANA: Personally I thought it was a little bit easier to be a little bit more creative. Yes, because you can have your ideas and put them on a piece of paper and colour them in and do that sort of thing and visualise it. But, when you're actually in there doing it per se you are actually immersed in it completely. So like you have the sound, the colour ... Just being inside the space and seeing all the different things you can accomplish and that made it personally a little bit easier for me to design things cause you could just see all your options.

KAREN: I think playing around with the textures is something you can't normally do. Like when you got [traditional] set design [in a box] you got paper, felt, or fabric and that pretty much about it. You go in there and you got wire, you got lights, you can paint with snow, so much more is accessible. And it's all at your fingertips … And it's like 'No, that doesn't work! Scrap it'. And you just hit the undo button or you get the erasure.

SALLY: Or you just pick it up and throw it away …

The students' insights into their learning VR also highlighted the technology's affordance of perspective-taking and how this was particularly well suited for learning about theatre design from the viewpoint of the director, actors (through the play's characters), and audience. They also pondered how Tilt Brush made them connect with the play's absurdist genre, understand the importance of symbolism to the genre, and deepened their understanding of set design to such a degree that it improved the production of their traditional cardboard set box which was a summative assessment task:

RESEARCHER: How do you think working in Tilt Brush helped you understand the play … and learning about different aspects of drama?

CHRIS: I think it helped all of us because we are basically coming from an audience perspective. We're looking at it. We're not just the creators of something on a piece of paper. We're basically sitting down like we're on a stage looking at this dark area and we have this piece of light (effect) and the costume or [elements of] the set design and we're able to see, 'Oh that doesn't look good [or] I don't understand what that means', and we're able to change it …

KAREN: I think it really worked with this style [of play]. I think absurdism was the one to do this with because it could be weird. Things are very symbolic in absurdism … If you were doing realism, I'm not sure how that would go [as] everything would have to be perfect. Everything would have to be a lot more structured.

SALLY: I feel like you could definitely do it but it could not be like a first experience [of design in VR]. Like we had a first experience and that worked with absurdism. But if we had more experience and knowledge on it [creation in VR] then you could definitely do other things …

LANA: Because the play is very much about stepping into their shoes [the characters] and experiencing what they felt and what happened to them, I think playing around with Tilt Brush and actually being there [amongst the set elements] made you open up your perspective a little bit more … You got to see it from the audience perspective but also from them [the characters] – how they felt at the time … like how Sylvie and Ray felt [the mother and father characters in the play].

KAREN: … If we were creating a set before [the VR experience] we might just say couch… there, this there – alright done. But when you go in and start to build around it [in VR] you're like, 'Ok that can't go there we need this over here'. Or, 'This makes more sense for it to be there'. So the depth of our actual set designs when we actually came to make the [traditional cardboard set] box version was so much more in depth than previous years because we've had this experience.

DEE: Like your reasoning for everything.

KAREN: Yeah.

DEE: We were thinking like directors.

LANA: I guess the point of anything is that you want to engage your audience. That's like the primary aspect when it comes to theatre and performance and from having this [VR] experience of being directors we had to think what was right. But if we were the audience what would we perceive it as? Like the way we could explore all the different possibilities made it easier to switch between both perspectives.

Even Anita who was initially very reluctant to use Tilt Brush for theatre design tempered her views at the conclusion of the unit of work. The following excerpt from a peer-to-peer interview illustrates Anita's shift in attitude towards using VR while providing insight into the (understandable) reluctance of some students to focus more on the creative product than to trust the creative process:

LANA: Did you have a negative or positive experience when you went into this VR space?

ANITA: A bit of both. I started quite negatively because I have done costume designing some time in the past in Year 8 and I did that on paper so I kinda knew about how to do it and I had a process of what I was going to do. So for Miss [Rowley] to say we are going to do it in VR, it was something I'd never done before and something that I just didn't know anything about – it was a bit frightening. The first time I did it, because I am kinda a bit of a perfectionist, I didn't kinda grasp the concept of it and I found myself trying to make everything perfect and in VR. It's kinda really hard to do that so I didn't really enjoy the costume designing part of it. But when it came to set design part I found it a lot more engaging. Well I like looking at other people's stuff just not my own work.

LANA: So did you feel a lot more creative in a sense because you could play around with a lot of different things but when it came to the underlying factors of it, you wanted to have the fine lines, the perfectionist side of it?

ANITA: You can do a lot more on it [Tilt Brush]. But it's just my skill levels is not that great and so I didn't really enjoy going in there because I just couldn't do it.

LANA: So was there like any underlying positive aspects that you actually liked about your VR experience.

ANITA: I think that it's very positive in the way you can actually do so much more stuff with it. Like your textures are different, you can add sound to stuff, you can change the background. Like there are so many different things that you can do that can create a really engaging um …

LANA: Opportunity?

ANITA: Yeah

LANA: So would you recommend VR to anyone?

ANITA: Definitely try it. I think everyone has their own opinion. Everyone should try it.

Anita's quest to achieve technically perfect designs was different from the other students who looked forward to the process of experimentation through serious play in Tilt Brush. Process-focused approaches can be considered risky in education, particularly in secondary schools, where the concept of learning through play is uncommon and where high-stakes standardised assessment requiring demonstration of technical proficiency is the norm. This quest for 'perfection' in learning extends beyond the preference of individual students. As Sahlberg (2016) points out this can narrow the 'freedom and flexibility in schools and classrooms to do things that are truly meaningful to (students). It also prevents teachers from experimentation, reduces the use of alternative pedagogical approaches, and limits risk-taking in schools and classrooms' (p. 135). No doubt it was a 'frightening' process for some students to be given the freedom to explore and experiment with an emerging technology. However, most students found concentrating on the creative process within Tilt Brush as a shared experience more valuable than producing an individual perfect end product.

'It's About All of Us Being in the Learning Space Together': Teacher Reflections on the iVR Project

The teaching team emphasised the benefits of the project for collaborative learning. This related to student peer group learning, teachers and students learning together, and the learning that took place in the teacher team that implemented and supported the project. The importance of working together in a teacher team with an unknown technology was considered vital not only for troubleshooting but for generating new ideas and directions for learning. Moreover, the teachers suggested that seeing teachers, especially those who had been in the profession for a long time, take a risk on using an emerging technology in the classroom had a knock-on effect to 'inspire' others to do the same:

RESEARCHER: So what's it like to work in a [teacher] team on a new project?

GILLIAN: I think it's exciting and really important to have that team because each person brings something different to the team …

LOUISE: It's building relationships between the staff. This is really great … Now I want to do more projects together.

DAVID: It gives you hundreds of ideas. We literally interrupt each other probably 3 or 4 times a day being like what if we did this, what if we did that? …

LOUISE: Now I'm looking at another elective in Year 9 called media and creative industries because of the excitement. And as one of the more experienced teachers of the staff, who's probably one of the oldest members of staff [If I] can take on this technology into my classroom it can inspire other teachers. I've already had [other teachers] come to me and say, 'How do you do that [use VR in class]?' and I say, 'Well I didn't really know what I was doing [with the VR] but I just did it.' And so another teacher has decided to introduce her classes to a computer program she's been too frightened to use but she's just jumped off the cliff with it and discovered what works and what doesn't work because I inspired her to try stuff.

Louise suggested that her willingness to be 'a bit brave' emerged from her preference for ongoing development of her teaching practice which was linked to a focus on improving student engagement and understanding. She also suggested that the risks of using Tilt Brush resonated with the signature pedagogies of drama teaching such as play, experimentation, improvisation, and trusting in the open-endedness of the creative process:

RESEARCHER: I know you say you are one of the oldest teachers on staff and I'm interested in why you would take a risk with VR?
LOUISE: I like new stuff … I never teach the same thing the same way twice. I'm always looking to improve my teaching and I start with what are the kids are going to need to learn … I constantly evaluate during any unit of work I do. Are the kids getting this? Is this going to get them to what I want them to understand? How can I engage them in their learning? And I think with this VR project I have been able to see how something that I've done for quite a few years, this Year 11 project on design, has now become so much bigger than it was in that the kids can talk about their directorial vision on a deeper level. That's engagement. That's higher order thinking skills. That's problem-solving. The stuff that's really important for the future and where we're at with education … It's about all of us being in the learning space together. We're together. Sometimes I'm the teacher, sometime they are the teacher. And being willing to do that. Not having the idea that you need to be in control of this whole process because you can see how someone would yell from the VR space, 'How do I get that to do this?' and someone will come and stand beside them and help. And it's not me. It's them [the students] … It fits really well with drama because we do play and experiment and improvise a lot to create. We never know what we are going to create when we start a play-building unit. We never know what it's going to end up like but we … trust the process will take you somewhere and where you end up you will never know what the answer is going to be but that's part of our creative pedagogy … I tell the kids trust the process, ideas will build on ideas. It will

get to the point where it will snowball. And you will be enjoying the creative ride as we go because that's what happens.

The teacher's observation on the benefits of students and teachers learning about the potential of an emerging technology together was echoed by Gillian who suggested that this approach promoted an active conception of learning. In this type of learning environment students exercised control and responsibility for their learning:

> Maybe instead of it being that regular teacher and learner relationship where the teacher leads, I think everybody learning together sort of promotes the idea to kids that learning is an active thing. Something they can do and help each other with. It's not something you wait for and the learning is just poured in. I think this project is something that has reached out to break through and [make] new boundaries altogether … The kids are more in control of their own learning and they take a bit more responsibility [for it].

Louise proposed that learning with iVR might best be situated within the pedagogical model of project-based learning and that good curriculum design was paramount to successful deployment of the technology in the classroom. She described the need for teachers to factor in extra time in projects using iVR so that students could master technical aspects and explore and experiment with the features of specific immersive environments:

> The process of taking their director's vision into the VR space allowed them [the students] to think more about the audience's experience and really immerse themselves in the director's role … In the design process there is a lot of experimentation and collaboration required. Tilt Brush has endless features that allow this to occur. Sketches could be saved, videoed, gifs made and photographed, and this process of documenting their ideas helped the students reflect on their ideas more. The quality of their ideas developed further … [Tilt Brush] incorporated many amazing creative features. Designs could be instantly erased and then re-created quickly. It had many resources that we do not usually have in the drama room. Endless colours and brushes, backgrounds, models to be imported and guides to draw around. Sketches could be made smaller or bigger in an instant … You have to be a bit brave, confident that you can work with your pedagogy to know where you might go with it … I think project based learning is where it's at because the nature of the VR is that you can only have the kid in there for a period of time. It's got to be an … element in a unit of work. You can't have 29 kids watching one kid in there. Mind you it is entertaining. And you've got to have the time to be able to do it because first of all they've got to learn how to use the controllers, how to use the headset, then they've got to learn what's in

that particular software program that you are using and once they get a little bit of mastery of that then they can go and start applying it to their project ... You need enough in a unit [of work] to keep them going when they are not in the VR – carefully planned and timed tasks that students can select and complete. It certainly took our learning to a deeper level because of what they had to think about before they went to create [in VR]. They had to know on a deeper level what their directorial vision was and they needed to know what they wanted to engage the audience with so [using VR] was certainly putting [their directorial vision] to the test and it was a good test because they have certainly come up with interesting stuff ...

Gillian and David offered similar observations on how Tilt Brush could engage learners to achieve content mastery:

GILLIAN: I've been blown away by how engaged and how busy the kids have been, and there's a real atmosphere of something exciting's happening. The students really seem to tackle the topic and at depth and really engage with each other and they have embraced the technology. It was new ... for a very short time but now it's sort of not about the technology but about what they are doing within the technology.

DAVID: One of the great things I remember is when Louise came to me and said, 'Music! Music! How do I get music [into Tilt Brush]?' So we came down. We had a play. And suddenly we are inside the thing and playing some music and suddenly all the brushes come alive and then the kids have taken that and gone further with it. Whole new levels have come alive.

Perhaps one of the most telling impacts of using iVR in the classroom was how it highlighted the hidden talents of more reserved students and enriched educational equity. There is long-standing substantial evidence of inequity in education for students from lower socioeconomic and rural and remote geographic background (Southgate, 2017). Giving students from these background access to emerging technologies is vital in closing gaps in educational outcomes. Louise elaborated on this:

[The VR project] has allowed all students to be equal. Once in the technology they were able to each contribute in a very real and tangible way to the group idea. *It also allowed our rural students to have access to quality programs, which can sometimes not be available to them because of location.* I think that it's quite empowering for the kids. Because they might come from a farm where they have no internet but they can create VR like the National Theatre in UK. There's no reason we can't lead technology learning from Dungog. They can be on the same playing field as a school in the city and to feel that our school is cutting edge in that way. It's actually bought out some kids.

Like people were saying, 'Oh my God I never knew Felix could draw'. Or, 'Have a look at what Elle's doing. Look at that. That's amazing.' And some of the kids that have not been so forthcoming of their talents in the drama classroom, who've been a little bit like shy little flowers in the corner, have really grown. And some of these kids, I know come from poorer socio-economic [backgrounds] with no internet at home, no quality computer at home, and they're being allowed to grow within their group because they have a shared responsibility for getting all those tasks done and they have really risen and I find that that's the leveller. It allows everyone to be on the same level playing field. So it doesn't matter if you've got all that stuff at home. You can access it here at school which is great for those kids. You can see that their whole faces have changed. The way they even carry themselves around the place. They walk in and they know they are an integral part of the team that is creating this thing, this directorial vision. And their ideas count. And that the egalitarian nature of it. No one's better than anyone else in there [Tilt Brush]. Everybody can have a go. And hey, if you make a mistake you just push a button and it disappears and you start again. So that's the great thing about it … I think their learning has accelerated … [and] I also think it's quite empowering for the teachers because you don't have to have all the answers before you start. (emphasis added)

Conclusion

While some students were initially 'freaked out' by the thought of learning drama through iVR, the small class size, access to enough VR equipment in a physical space large enough to use it in a fully embodied way, and the many affordances of Tilt Brush, smoothed the way for a unique and productive educational experience. Both students and teachers suggested the iVR experience had strengthened engagement and enriched learning to allow student to exceed curriculum outcomes. The learning affordances of Tilt Brush enabled students to meet the learning objectives of perceptively and creatively understanding and manipulating theatrical elements and of deepening their knowledge of how directors and designers communicate meaning in theatre to engage the audience. Students developed a deep understanding of the learning affordances of Tilt Brush through a combination of ongoing teacher-guided activity and by the sequencing and pacing of the unit of work which encouraged play.

Every aspect of the Deeper Learning model (Noguera, Darling-Hammond, and Friedlaender, 2015), from the development of content mastery, effective communication, critical thinking and problem-solving, collaboration, self-directed learning, and an academic mindset, were abundantly evident in the way students went about the formative assessment task to conceptualise and realise sophisticated directorial visions in iVR. Students work in iVR was not isolated to the immersive world. The virtual studio and the physical space of the drama classroom merged as higher order thinking about genre, symbolism, and perspective-taking in theatre manifested in 2D and 3D form. The process of working in a sandbox iVR environment positively influenced their more traditional written work on directorial vision and the cardboard set boxes that students created at the end of the unit of work.

Student creativity is inextricably linked to opportunities for peer collaboration and evaluation and teacher's affirmative attitudes towards flexibility, choice, autonomy and open-ended possibility:

> There is strong evidence from across the curriculum and age-range that where children and young people are given some control over their learning and supported to take risks with the right balance between structure and freedom, their creativity is enhanced. (Davies, Jindal-Snape, Collier, Digby, Hay, and Howe, 2013, p. 85)

Crucially, a set of interconnected pedagogical approaches and dynamics structured and supported the use of the technology in the classroom. The first of these was the teacher team approach to pushing the possibilities of iVR for learning. The classroom teacher's curious disposition, commitment to improving the student experience of learning, and deep curriculum expertise and pedagogical knowledge meant that the experimental nature of using of iVR in the classroom was not considered an imposition but rather an extension of practice (albeit a 'brave' and unconventional choice). Significantly, the classroom teacher leveraged the signature pedagogies of drama education by: weaving iVR through the stages of the creative process and scaffolding students to trust in the openness of the method; structuring connected collaborative tasks inside *and* outside of iVR; and improvising on the immersive task expectation by shifting the focus from product to process. Most importantly, the teachers were willing to accept that they were learners too and that there was much to gained as professionals and members of a school community by 'being in the learning space together' with their students. This reflected a non-technicised conception of pedagogy that fully supported students 'freedom and flexibility in … [the] classrooms to do things that were truly meaningful to them' (Sahlberg, 2016, p. 135).

The broader potential for the technology to elevate the talented yet reserved students was demonstrated. Moreover, the significance of giving rural students early access to an emerging technology cannot be understated. There are profound equity implication in patterns of access to technologies and especially emerging ones. Low-income school communities, including those located in rural areas, are rarely given an opportunity to lead in the emerging technology-enhanced learning space. They are restricted from doing so because of lack of resources and geographic isolation from the latest Edtech trends and professional learning accompanying these. The virtual studio of Tilt Brush offered rural students, who had very limited material and digital resources at home, endless possibilities for exploration and creation that could deepen their interest in and understanding of theatrical design. As the classroom teacher pointed out, even if students came from a farm where they had no internet and limited access to quality computing, they were able to come to school and use the virtual studio of Tilt Brush in ways that resonated with cutting-edge international projects on immersive theatre. One of the most significant lesson of the Dungog High School VR School Study was the prospect of using iVR for learning to level the playing field of privilege.

References

Board of Studies NSW. (2009). *Drama stage 6 syllabus*. Sydney: Board of Studies NSW.

Botella, M., Zenasni, F., & Lubart, T. (2018). What are the stages of the creative process? What visual art students are saying. *Frontiers in Psychology*, 9 (Art. 2266), 1–13. doi:10.3389/fpsyg.2018.02266

Cameron, M. (2005). *Ruby Moon*. Sydney: Currency Press.

Davies, D., Jindal-Snape, D., Collier, C., Digby, R., Hay, P., & Howe, A. (2013). Creative learning environments in education – a systematic literature review. *Thinking Skills and Creativity*, 8, 80–91. doi:10.1016/j.tsc.2012.07.004

Davis, S. (2015). Liveliness mediation and immediacy – Innovative technology use in process and performance. In M. Anderson, D. Cameron, & P. Sutton (Eds.), *Innovation, technology and converging practices in drama education and applied theatre* (pp. 33–48). London and New York: Routledge.

Kozar, O. (2010). Towards better group work: Seeing the difference between cooperation and collaboration. *English Teaching Forum*, 48(2), 16–23.

Lusted, D. (1986). Why pedagogy? *Screen*, 27(5), 2–16. doi:10.1093/screen/27.5.2

Makransky, G., Terkildsen, T. S., & Mayer, R. E. (2019). Adding immersive virtual reality to a science lab simulation causes more presence but less learning. *Learning and Instruction*, 60, 225–236. doi:10.1016/j.learninstruc.2017.12.007

Mayer, R. E., & Moreno, R. (2003). Nine ways to reduce cognitive load in multimedia learning. *Educational Psychologist*, 38(1), 43–52. doi:10.1207/S15326985EP3801_6

Noguera, P., Darling-Hammond, L., & Friedlaender, D. (2015). Equal opportunity for Deeper Learning. Jobs for the future. Retrieved https://files.eric.ed.gov/fulltext/ED560802.pdf

Sahlberg, P. (2016). The global educational reform movement and its impact on schooling. In K. Mundy, A. Green, B. Lingard, & A. Verger (Eds.), *Handbook of global education policy* (pp. 128–144). Oxford: John Wiley & Sons.

Southgate, E. (2017). *Fair connection to professional careers: Understanding social difference and disadvantage, institutional dynamics and technological opportunities*. Perth: NCSEHE. Retrieved https://www.ncsehe.edu.au/wp-content/uploads/2017/09/Southgate_Fa ir-connection-to-professional-careers.pdf

Sweller, J. (1988). Cognitive load during problem solving: Effects on learning. *Cognitive Science*, 12(2), 257–285. doi:10.1016/0364-0213(88)90023-7

Sweller, J. (2005). Implications of cognitive load theory for multimedia learning. In R. Mayer & R. E. Mayer (Eds.), *The Cambridge handbook of multimedia learning* (pp. 19–30). Cambridge: Cambridge University Press.

Weisberg, D. S., Hirsh-Pasek, K., Golinkoff, R. M., Kittredge, A. K., & Klahr, D. (2016). Guided play: Principles and practices. *Current Directions in Psychological Science*, 25(3), 177–182. doi:10.1177%2F0963721416645512

8

SCHOOLING VIRTUAL FUTURES

What We Need to Know and Do to Ensure Powerful Learning Through Immersive Virtual Reality

Introduction

There is no other technology like iVR. It can transport a person to an artificial world which envelops their senses to such a degree that they feel as though they are really there. For this reason, iVR offers immense potential for learning *and* distinct ethical risks especially related to the developmental stage/s of the child. Decades of research on screen-based VR has provided valuable empirical and theoretical insights into learning with the technology; however, as a commercially young technology, there is still is still much to discover about using iVR in different school communities, with diverse groups of students, and through different modes of delivery. In particular, educators need educating on the technical properties and learning affordances of iVR. This will enable a shift in the collective conversation where pedagogical questions can be foregrounded. A central premise of this book is that teachers should shift from asking 'What equipment and/or software should my school invest in?' to engaging with the more pedagogically informed questions of 'What are the learning affordances of iVR and how can these be used to create educational opportunities that are not readily accessible or different from those currently available for my students?' Educators should ask the EdTech industry to show them the evidence that iVR is developmentally appropriate for students and that it is effective for different types of learning *across* subject areas of the curriculum. It is true that new kinds of technology-enhanced learning are implemented ahead of the development of an evidence base; however, this does not negate the necessity for the teaching profession, industry, and academia to work together in earnest to investigate the uses of iVR in classrooms that extend well beyond giving students a novelty experience.

This final chapter provides an overview of the current state-of-play of research on iVR and school education drawing together research literature with the findings from the VR School Study. It then goes on to outline what we still need to know to ensure iVR is used in schools for Deeper Learning (Noguera, Darling-Hammond, and Friedlaender, 2015). This is followed by a suggested set of actions in the areas of initial teacher education, in-service teacher professional learning (sometimes known as professional development), and for design of and research into the use of immersive virtual learning environments in schools.

What We Know About iVR and School Education

While there are several decades of research on learning in virtual environment through screen-based VR, research on using iVR in a range of educational settings including schools is in its infancy. Early theoretical literature on the learning affordances of 3D virtual learning environments (Dalgarno and Lee, 2010) remains relevant to iVR. The concept of learning affordances provides educators with a lens to interrogate how the specific features of virtual environments can facilitate learning in ways that are markedly different to traditional pedagogy or other forms of technology-enhanced learning. The embodied, active learning that iVR can offer amplifies the potential of these learning affordances. For example, in screen-based VR you can interact in first-person mode; however, in 6DOF multi-user iVR environment that interaction is palpably immediate as a user can pick up virtual objects, manipulate them, hand then to others in the virtual space, and even travel through worlds in various modes from walking, swimming, and flying. It is actually like 'being there' in the world with others in an engagingly (and sometimes uncomfortable) visceral way. Similarly, manipulating size and scale in screen-based virtual environments is certainly fun and Winn's (1993) example of the learning affordance of transduction, where a learner swims in a droplet of water and is the same size as its microorganisms, is certainly educationally potent. However, the power of the educational experience should exponentially increase if those organisms are all around the learner and they are able to pick up the organism, pull it apart to learn about its constitute elements, or manipulate the conditions under which the microorganism lives to experience its immediate changes in an immersive fashion, or become that microorganism and go on a natural journey as if in the first person.

The trouble is that at present we just do not know enough about using iVR for efficacious learning, in all its various manifestations, and with diverse groups of students within specific educational contexts. The literature on screen-based VR indicates that the technology is good for procedural learning and can enhance understanding of spatial concepts. This finding is likely to translate to the use of the iVR technology in school subjects that seek to develop these types of knowledge and skills. Far less is known about using iVR technology to promote higher order thinking, collaboration, communication, and problem-solving skills in both adult and school education (Jensen and Konradsen, 2018).

This gap in knowledge about using iVR to develop aspects of Deeper Learning was a key impetus for the VR School Study which features in this book. The research was also driven by a need to understand the ethical, practical, and pedagogical implications of embedding this emerging technology, with its unique affordances, technical and spatial requirements, in school classrooms. Moving iVR research from tightly controlled laboratories to the dynamic and often unpredictable natural settings of the classroom will be vital if we are to appreciate how learning can be choreographed and unfold in virtual environments: 'Scaling up' the use of the technology in schools will need to be on the back of credible evidence based on research in natural educational settings.

The VR School Study highlighted the need to develop a middle-order theory of the pedagogy of iVR. It was from insights derived from using iVR in school classrooms that the middle-range theoretical APIL framework (Table 3.1 in chapter 3) was borne. APIL attempts to disentangle some of the major issues that confront teachers when choosing, using, and evaluating the deployment of iVR in their classroom. The framework poses a set of instructional and technical questions to guide educators' decision to teach with iVR. If APIL is a pragmatic framework, the two scaffolds developed to underpin it aimed to provide a more conceptual approach to disrupting some of the commonly held assumptions about education through iVR.

The first scaffold (Table 3.2 in chapter 3) challenged the simplistic yet pervasive dichotomous categorisation of iVR experiences as either passive or active, replacing this overly simplistic dichotomy with a pedagogical typology of iVR that incorporated notions of embodied interaction and ability to impact on and have some autonomy over learning in/with virtual environments. This typology challenges a naive view that putting on a VR headset will result in singular type of immersive pedagogical experience and although it presents a series of idealised categorical forms it is flexible enough to explain the pedagogical potential of hybrid applications that may incorporate aspects of different types of iVR. The non-hierarchical typology illustrates that *pedagogically* iVR is not one thing and that educators need to come to grips with how different types of iVR environments (through the combination of hardware and software affordances) can enable different types of learning experiences. The typology, while derived from years of observation, will need empirical testing and refinement especially as the evidence on learning through iVR grows and theories of embodied cognition are tested.

The second scaffold (Figure 3.2 in chapter 3) challenges some well-worn tropes in technology-enhanced learning such as 'tech-as-tool' and 'pedagogy before technology'. This scaffold asks educators to critically evaluate iVR environments for pedagogical approaches that are already infused into applications and ask if these are appropriate for the curriculum, and a philosophy of education that seeks to empower human flourishing for the good of the individual, the social collective, and the planet. This scaffold suggests that while a virtual environment may be used as tool for learning, there are alternative framings especially when iVR applications are used as a medium for expressive content creation and as a holistic 'total' learning environment which can allows for many and varied learning activities to take place in VR and outside of it.

The VR School Study built on previous experimental research which underscored the need to consider the developmental appropriateness and ethical implications of using the technology with children (Segovia and Bailenson, 2009; Stanford University Virtual Human Interaction Lab, 2011). We simply do not know what the long term effects of immersion on children and young people will be. Nor do we properly understand how children and young people physiologically and psychologically experience strong feelings of presence that highly iVR can produce. This warranted a cautious approach to embedding iVR in school classrooms. The VR School Study produced clear protocols and resources to assist with the ethical use of iVR in classrooms including information for informed parental consent and child assent, a teacher script, and a classroom poster to mitigate the possibility of cybersickness and other physical harms (Figure 5.4 in chapter 5), and a procedure to guide students and staff on respectful interaction when using iVR (Figure 5.5 in chapter 5). Teachers should also be aware that boys are probably more likely to have tried iVR than girls and that some girls may find it embarrassing to wear the headset and feel discomfort because a headset stops them seeing what is going on in the outside world. A respectful and supportive approach is required in this situation.

Furthermore, the study clearly illustrated that it was not the pedagogical imaginations of teachers or students which acted as a barrier to smooth classroom implementation. Rather, the main barriers were: the difficulties of finding classroom spaces large enough to accommodate even modest play areas required for several units of iVR equipment; equity issues related to limited access to enough quality computing devices (either owned by the school or BYOD); and a lack of technical reliability of iVR equipment and constraints of the school internet network. This resonated with other research which found that teachers considered the technical set-up of highly IVR as a barrier to everyday use in the classroom (Laine, 2019).

One of the clearest pedagogical findings from the study was that teachers can successfully leverage the signature pedagogies (Shulman, 2005) of their subject area to create units of work that use sandbox virtual environments to promote Deeper Learning for students (Noguera, Darling-Hammond, and Friedlaender, 2015). The study indicated that it is possible to devote a modest amount of time to introduce a self-directed learning task using iVR in the science classroom with less time given over to explicit teaching and have students achieve content mastery at the same level as those who only experienced a traditional pedagogical approach. This finding is relevant in an era where curriculum is overcrowded and teachers may question whether it is worth introducing a new technology for learning into their classrooms. Teachers need to plan for those students who are unable to use iVR because of pre-existing physical or psychological reasons or because they are prone to cybersickness or express discomfort in immersive environments.

The VR School research responded to the matter of learner engagement in the context of 'no code create' sandboxes that supply both an amazing set of content creation tools and a dazzling array of potential distractions. As educators it is worth asking ourselves if we would be able to concentrate on undertaking a serious learning task if we were transported to an unsupervised wonderland where anything was possible – swimming with dolphins, flying with friends over mountains, burrowing underground, jumping off clouds into a crystal clear lake or riding alpacas? The research, even with its imperfect data capture, suggested that most students spent around two-thirds of their time undertaking the learning task when in highly iVR, with many groups staying on-task 80% or more of the time. While there was variability in on-task engagement, this result suggests that highly iVR can be used to develop self-directed learning, a valuable asset of 21st century learning.

The iVR formative assessment tasks that the teachers developed for the units of work in both case studies called for higher order thinking (Krathwohl, 2002) and an academic mindset characterised by perseverance. That students persisted with the assessment tasks despite the cognitive challenges of collaboratively undertaking new content acquisition, needing to constantly problem solve when prototyping, and having to master a new technology and its creative and communicative features all within a context at some schools where the equipment regularly failed and interrupted learning. Students moved well and truly beyond understanding the novelty aspects of the technology with most students' work samples in and about iVR exemplifying all aspects of Deeper Learning.

Interestingly, it was not the teachers but the students from the VR School Study who provided the most insightful responses to the central pedagogical questions of this book – What are the learning affordances of iVR applications and how can these be used to create educational opportunities that are not readily accessible or different from those currently available for students? Students described the joys of working together on learning tasks in an embodied, *first-person* mode in multi-user 'no code create' sandbox virtual environment. The ability to enter a different world and create their very own part of it with others provided an immediacy, authenticity, and sense of control over learning in a way that was qualitatively different from screen-mediated VR or other traditional collaborative classroom activities. The unmediated first-person experience of iVR for development of set and costume design bought alive the different perspectives of actor, director, and audience in theatre studies. Furthermore the *natural semantics* of iVR were beneficial in allowing drama students to evoke and easily manipulate the mood of a directorial vision by easily changing the music, 'skybox' colour/mood, texture and size and position of virtual objects, allowing them to *feel* the differences that design decisions can make for audiences and actors in a more visceral way than looking at a small static cardboard set box could.

Students emphasised that *manipulation of size and scale* was key to developing a deeper understanding of content knowledge associated with the learning task. Being able to make an interactive skyscraper of a brain or a model of an eye that could be toured with a rollercoaster or a stomach in which learners could slosh around in the gastric juice required systematic research translated through a creative process that utilised manipulation of size and scale to facilitate the learning of others who could experience the body organ. There is no equivalent embodied, interactive, and agentic experience available in a school classroom.

This type of manipulation was linked to the creative representation of quite abstract ideas or *reification*. Reification refers to transforming relatively an abstract idea into a perceptible representation. For example, the concept of directorial vision was initially abstract to students. When students were asked to develop a directorial vision for the play they were studying and represent it for others to experience, they used the tools of the iVR sandbox to construct an experience that drew on the dynamic interplay of lighting/mood, colour, texture, music, and layers of symbols woven into animated virtual objects. It is not possible for schools or even most theatre companies to experiment with prototyping directorial vision by iterating through fully realised actual set designs that a director, actor, or audience member can navigate through and interact in/with.

The learning affordance of *transduction* or extending the ability to grasp or feel data that is usually beyond the immediate senses was evident in the way students utilised iVR to create models of body organs that could be experienced externally and internally. When students made their model of a human heart that allowed the user to travel through it in the direction of the flow of blood through its internal chambers they were evoking a feel for factual information related to the structure and function of the organ. The experience of this in immersive mode supplemented by the annotated 'fun facts' about the heart strategically placed along the journey made it a unique and powerful learning experience for both the students who created the model and the learner experiencing it.

Students emphasised that having access to highly iVR equipment and sandbox applications increased their sense of autonomy over the learning process and encouraged them to be creative and collaborative because they were able to enter another world where only their commitment to research and collective imaginations could limit them in realising their vision which came to life right before their eyes. This was captured in student comments that the technology allowed them to 'actually interact with the things you are learning about' and 'bring what's going on in your mind to life!'

In both case studies the teachers' units of work were structured to make the most of the active and agentic learning potential of 'no code create' sandbox iVR environments. Furthermore, the technology was viewed as a means of increasing more equitable access to new types of learning and resources that were not readily available to their students from low income and rural communities. In the case of the rural school it was also viewed as a way to bridge a geographic chasm by having students who had limited access to the theatre use the same technology for creative purposes as some of the most innovative theatre companies in the world.

What We Need to Know and Do to Enable a Bright Future for iVR Learning in Schools

Fostering a productive future for iVR in schools will take a concerted effort across various fields and with many different types of stakeholders involved. Schools need to know if it is worth investing not inconsiderable amounts of time and money into the technology beyond a sale's pitch about appearing to be innovative. This section outlines several areas for more sustained action, and, while not exhaustive, it does attempt to clearly explicate areas that require attention and points of potential tension that may emerge.

Firstly, it is not good enough to make the case that children are already using iVR for leisure gaming and so the technology is relatively safe and appropriate. Ethical experimental research is required to determine the episodic and long-itudinal effects of immersion on children and young people and to better understand the technology's interaction with cognitive, affective, social, and moral developmental domains. Using a technology for learning at school should not make a student feel sick or cause physical or psychological discomfort. More research is required on cybersickness and other potential harms that iVR may cause children and young people. Experimental research on using iVR to understand immersive learning and embodied cognition and to improve the educational design of the technology is vital; however, state-of-the-art laboratory inquiry needs to be accompanied by state-of-the-actual research conducted when iVR is embedded within natural educational settings.

Research on using the technology in schools needs to be co-designed with teachers, a rare occurrence in either the screen-based (Mikropoulos and Natsis, 2011) or immersive VR education literature. Co-designing research and con-ducting research with teachers and students in actual classrooms will open up the field to a myriad of unexplored ethical, technical, design, pedagogical, and learning questions, and it will increase the depth, credibility, and generalisability of research findings. Moreover, the validity of findings will be increased if diverse populations of students participate in research and working genuinely with the teaching profession in schools will ensure this.

The pedagogy of iVR requires intensive theoretical development and empirical inquiry inclusive of but beyond concepts from learning science. While pedagogy is often implied in iVR education research, it is rarely clearly explicated, philo-sophically elaborated on, or documented in the field. It is not just a case of looking at what teachers think of and do with the technology in classrooms but of the pedagogical potential that is imbued in the combination of hardware and software: In other words, what types of learning the technology can enable once teachers understand how they can leverage their pedagogical expertise (and sig-nature pedagogies) to create unique, engaging tasks to facilitate aspects of Deeper Learning. In research terms and practice, there is the heady brew of elements that need to coalesce in order to investigate the true potential of iVR for learning. It can include the use of a virtual experience as a stimulus or supplementary lesson activity but it largely involves extending the use of iVR to active learning tasks involving higher order thinking and which scaffolded self-directed learning. Bringing together a non-technicised conception of pedagogy, its relationship to aspects of Deeper Learning, the pedagogical typology (Table 3.2 in chapter 3) and a range of research methodologies will facilitate meaningful, systematic, and comparative scholarly exploration of the pedagogy of iVR across subject area of the curriculum.

Specifically, research needs to account for different modes of delivery of iVR across subject areas and not just in STEM. We need to better understand how schools are incorporating the technology for learning – in classrooms, labs, libraries, maker-spaces, and through excursions to VR arcades. We need to investigate the impact of different opportunities to use iVR on learning and learners and we need to be alert to gender dynamics especially where access to the technology is limited to labs and ICT elective subjects which are often only attractive to boys. Furthermore, it is worth mentioning that while this book has been about embedding iVR in classrooms in a curriculum-aligned way, the public pedagogy of iVR continues to grow. This include informative iVR applications on history, science, and literature available for download from game stores, and destination-based iVR education applications provided at institutions such as museums, art galleries and public libraries. The pedagogical approach of developers and providers of iVR educational experiences in the public domain deserves more scholarly attention. Indeed, instructional design has long been influenced by recreational game development. Hence, there is a need for continued investigation on how to leverage the best of immersive interaction and navigation techniques and game mechanics with learning science, theories of embodied cognition and pedagogical theory to inform the design of effective iVR learning environments.

At a mundane but important level, there are a number of technical and practical issues to solve if iVR is to be seamlessly embedded into classrooms. Teachers and students must be able to easily set up individual and class accounts required to run iVR applications and have the technology function reliably within the constraints of a school network. There is nothing more demotivating for a teacher than having to set up multiple accounts for a class, engineer a complex work-around to access a multi-user virtual environment, and having to spend considerable time troubleshooting technology failure when they should be facilitating learning. Similarly, students can become demotivated when the technology is consistently unreliable. The introduction of streaming platforms will no doubt put a strain on some schools' network and may hinder adoption unless companies supply technical solutions to alleviate the issue. No doubt the robustness of the technology for classroom use will improve over time; however, even the simpler set-up of all-in-one VR headsets still present spatial challenges for schools. Although these headsets do not require external positional tracking devices to be set up, reasonably large play areas are still needed for full interaction capability and enjoyment and the size and layout of the average classroom, designed for industrial age education, cannot accommodate this. Closely supervising students in iVR is recommended because potential cybersickness or other adverse reactions can be spotted early and an intervention can occur if students appear to ignore the Guardian system because they are so immersed in what they are doing. From a design perspective it would be useful to have a sound warning inside and outside VR which can signal when students leave a Guardian zone because visual cues may be inadequate for safety.

Educating pre-service teachers and the teaching profession about the technical and pedagogical potential of different types of iVR is vital. This is a tricky proposition for a number of reasons. Firstly, the low hanging fruit of pre-packaged kits with teacher-led tours that entails limited active learning from students beyond remembering and understanding factual knowledge has been understandably popular even it represents a limited use of the technology for learning. As Winn (1993) remarked more than two decades ago, the power of VR is wasted if it is used to simulate what was real; its power is in highlighting what might otherwise not be revealed and in allowing the learner to enact agency within the experience. It takes depth of technical and pedagogical expertise to select an iVR application with the right types of learning affordances that can be deployed within a unit of work in a sustained way to enhance higher order thinking and provide opportunities for students to develop and demonstrate skills such as collaboration and problem-solving. Learning about iVR in initial teacher education or through teacher professional development will involve bringing together bodies of knowledge on: (1) developmentally appropriate, ethical, and safe use; (2) basics of technical specifications of hardware and software; (3) conceptions of learning affordances and different types of iVR; and (4) classroom cases that demonstrate how existing pedagogical knowledge and signature pedagogies can be leveraged to utilise the technology to create Deeper Learning opportunities. This goes well beyond vendors offering demonstrations or pre-packaged professional learning experiences. We need to scope out where courses on immersive learning might fit within initial teacher education curriculum and for teacher professional learning requirements and accreditation standards.

While outside the remit of this book, robust research needs to be conducted on impacts of using immersive simulations for training pre-service and in-service teachers in the intricacies of instructional strategies, classroom management, and even managing relationships with parents and carers. The efficacy and transfer of skills learnt by interacting with virtual characters manipulated by real people in real time or through virtual pedagogical agents powered by artificial intelligence (AI) in immersive training environments will require close scholarly attention.

Finally, policy advice is required to inform teachers about the legal implications of using iVR. This includes copyright and privacy issues related to the creation of 360 content. Continued attention needs to be paid to the privacy policies of iVR hardware and software manufacturers to ensure that teachers and students are aware of the type of data that can and is being collected about them, and in particular any biometric data that is being harvested through positional and eye tracking technology. It is imperative that the privacy and pedagogical implications of AI-infused iVR applications be immediately addressed. The implications of algorithmically 'nudging' students via pedagogical agents or other opaque means in virtual worlds warrants serious ethical and educational attention. The only applications of this type that should be used in schools are those that clearly demonstrate adherence to human rights principles, have robust evidence of learning efficacy, and operate within systems which maintain the highest standards of consent, privacy, transparency, and accountability (Southgate et al., 2019). The history of AI bias and its negative consequences on human dignity and fair treatment highlights the need for vigilance, interdisciplinary collaboration, legislation, and regulation in this space. Finally, the profound digital equity issues evident in many schooling systems requires much more serious policy attention if all students, regardless of the family they were born into or the type of school they attend, are to have fair opportunities to access the benefits of immersive learning.

Teleporting Away (For Now)

As this book draws to its close there is one important recommendation I would make to educators and that is to try out as many types of headsets and iVR applications as possible. iVR is an experiential technology: Writing a book about the technology can never do justice to its experiential wonders or provide the types of embodied first-person insights that are required to make pedagogically sound decisions. It is worth exploring iVR from modest swivel experiences to highly interactive, multi-user environments because each will deepen a pedagogical understanding of how the technology can best be leveraged in developmentally appropriate ways for powerful learning.

Even if, after a thorough exploration of iVR, an educator decides that they don't personally like the experience, this is still valuable knowledge. Some students will feel exactly the same way and this will help educators to better evaluate iVR hardware and software applications for their class and identify ways to better integrate the technology and its alternatives in class. Curiosity and a desire for discovery are central to learning and these dispositions which will serve educators well when embarking on a pedagogical adventure through iVR.

References

Dalgarno, B., & Lee, M. J. (2010). What are the learning affordances of 3-D virtual environments? *British Journal of Educational Technology*, 41(1), 10–32. doi:10.1111/j.1467-8535.2009.01038.x

Jensen, L., & Konradsen, F. (2018). A review of the use of virtual reality head-mounted displays in education and training. *Education and Information Technologies*, 23(4), 1515–1529. doi:10.1007/s10639-017-9676-0

Krathwohl, D. R. (2002). A revision of Bloom's taxonomy: An overview. *Theory into Practice*, 41(4), 212–218. doi:10.1207/s15430421tip4104_2

Laine, J. (2019). Virtual field trip project: Affordances and user experiences of virtual reality technology in actual school settings. Retrieved https://helda.helsinki.fi/bitstream/handle/10138/300321/Laine_Joakim_Pro_gradu_2019.pdf?sequence=2

Mikropoulos, T. A., & Natsis, A. (2011). Educational virtual environments: A ten-year review of empirical research (1999–2009). *Computers & Education*, 56(3), 769–780. doi:10.1016/j.compedu.2010.10.020

Noguera, P., Darling-Hammond, L., & Friedlaender, D. (2015). Equal opportunity for Deeper Learning. Jobs for the future. Retrieved https://files.eric.ed.gov/fulltext/ED560802.pdf

Segovia, K., & Bailenson, J. (2009). Virtually true: Children's acquisition of false memories in virtual reality. *Media Psychology*, 12(4), 371–393. doi:10.1080/15213260903287267

Shulman, L. (2005). Signature pedagogies in the professions. *Daedalus*, 134(3), 52–59. https://www.jstor.org/stable/20027998

Southgate, E., Blackmore, K., Pieschl, S., Grimes, S., McGuire, J., & Smithers, K. (2019). *Artificial intelligence and emerging technologies in schools: A research report*. Australian Government: Department of Education. Retrieved https://docs-edu.govcms.gov.au/node/53008

Stanford University Virtual Human Interaction Lab. (2015). Virtual experiences can cause false memory formation in children. Retrieved https://vhil.stanford.edu/news/2011/virtual-experiences-can-cause-false-memory-formation-in-children/

Winn, W. (1993). *A conceptual basis for educational applications of virtual reality. Technical Publication R-93–9*. Human Interface Technology Laboratory of the Washington Technology Center. Seattle: University of Washington. Retrieved https://cittadinanzadigitale.wikispaces.com/file/view/1993_winn.pdf/34997779/1993_winn.pdf

INDEX

Page references in **bold** indicate a table; page references in *italics* indicate a figure.